What professionals are saying about *Accelerate Your Impact*

"JJ's objective is to create A Playbook for Professional Women to make their goals a reality and she completely nails it. A must read for every professional woman AND for every man who manages, works for or with women. If an organization wants a complete how-to guide to enable women to thrive this is the book."
> —Jeffery Tobias Halter, President YWomen; Author of *Why Women: The Leadership Imperative to Advancing Women and Engaging Men*

"JJ shares wisdom of overcoming standard patterns of behavior in order to unleash our potential to do phenomenal things in the world. Her motivating exploration into the empowerment of women—the empowerment of ourselves—is not only a great refresher for those in the trenches of the business world, but also a must read for young women entering the workforce. Pick this up for yourselves, your daughters and recent graduates—it won't disappoint."
> —Mel McGee, CEO, We Can Code IT

"The passion JJ has for pushing women to thrive in the workplace shines through in every word. So many women cannot articulate why they are 'stuck' in their career and JJ has helped with her simple focus on how our diversity and gender makes us great! Whether personal or career everyone needs to 'stretch themselves' to manifest what one desires!"
> —Jennifer Kirkpatrick, Dir, US Enterprise Flexible Consumption Models, Cisco Systems Inc.

"JJ hit the nail on the head that personal change is daunting. I was very impressed with how she identified challenges and assimilated tactics into a simplistic game plan. Stretching the risk muscle is something that we all need to put into practice!"
> —Dana Jacks, President, Data Strategy

*"**Accelerate Your Impact** is a brilliant road map for anyone seeking real-world examples and inspiration as we contemplate how to leave a meaningful footprint from our life's work. JJ, yet again, weaves her personal journey with best practices and proven outcomes. Her honest and straightforward style makes this the go-to book for today's professional."*
> —Tim Mueller, CEO, Global IT M&A Forum

*"JJ's passion for helping women achieve a competitive advantage is evident in this action-based step-by-step guide to **Accelerate Your Impact**. She artfully combines research and personal experience with exercises professional women can leverage to create a path for personal development. JJ will leave you feeling confident to take your career to the next step with the tools you will learn from this thoughtful playbook."*
—Lisa Parrott, Ph.D., USMC Veteran

*"**Accelerate Your Impact** is a thought-provoking collection of strategies that can help you achieve and exceed your professional goals. JJ shares her vast experiences and words of wisdom—this book is packed with actionable advice for those looking to take their impact to the next level."*
—Ellen Boehm, Business Operations Leader & Electrical Engineer, *Fortune* 500 company

*"**Accelerate Your Impact** is a comprehensive, straightforward and inspirational guide to illuminate opportunities to supercharge every women's career journey. This book has the power to inspire and transform and offers ideas and wisdom that can be applied directly to any woman's life. The content is organized in a way that meets every reader where they are in their journey and allows them to integrate learning in ways that matter most for them at various points in their career. It helps every women become the author of her destiny and encourages networking and collaboration to help others in their journey. It will be one of the most heavily highlighted and dog-eared books on my shelf!"*
—Sarah J. Mihalik, Vice President of Solutions, IBM Watson Health

*"JJ is a longtime WITI member, speaker and champion of women in tech and STEM-related careers. Her new book, **Accelerate Your Impact**, is a must read! Its unique insights and information will help all readers create a road map to reach and surpass their professional goals!"*
—David Leighton, President, WITI (Women In Technology International)

"JJ helps you understand that sponsorship must be earned, and is often recognized by delivering outstanding performance, consistent loyalty and a recognized personal brand."
—Sheryl Chamberlain, VP, Capgemini Group Strategic Initiatives and Partners

"JJ is a prolific author and adviser to the women in the high tech industry trying to find their 'sea legs' and who are also climbing the very complex corporate ladder. She has a stylistic persona that is easily understood by many of her women followers, both virtually and now in her new book. I read every word knowing that I did not want to miss one sentence of self-reflection and advice from JJ, a true mentor to myself and many others."

—Carole Cameron Inge, Ed.D., President and CEO,
Institute for the Commercialization of Technology

"It's no secret that we have too few women leaders in the boardroom and C-suite. Using the valuable strategies and insights JJ shares, more of us can elevate our leadership skills and step to the next level of success. If you aspire to become a high-value leader, this book will help you forge your path."

—Amy Franko, Founder and President, Impact Instruction Group

*"JJ poses tough questions in **Accelerate Your Impact**. Though tough, they are important, and powerfully introspective. As a business coach and adviser, I found her dive into relevance right on target, as it is the key to one's competitive edge in any business environment. For the entrepreneur, brand (relevance) is everything and is clearly the differentiator. With today's competitive business climate, connection to reality is more important than ever. This book will challenge your thinking and motivate the serious seeker to move forward. I recommend keeping it handy for a reference when facing your next business challenge."*

—Jan Conrad, Director, The Women's Business Center of Ohio, Cleveland

OTHER TITLES BY JJ DIGERONIMO

The Working Woman's GPS
Before You Say Yes

Accelerate Your Impact
Action-based strategies
to pave your professional path

By JJ DiGeronimo

SMART BUSINESS® BOOKS
An Imprint of Smart Business® Network Inc.

Published by Smart Business Books
An imprint of Smart Business Network Inc.
835 Sharon Drive, Suite 200
Westlake, OH 44145

Printed in the United States of America
Editor: Mark Scott and April Grasso
Interior Design: April Grasso
Cover Design: Jim Mericsko

ISBN: 978-0-9964080-6-6
Library of Congress Control Number: 2016939044

*To all the women who have made it possible
for us to spread our wings both professionally
and personally, you have blessed us in so many ways.*

*To all the fabulous women who make the time to read,
participate and contribute to Tech Savvy Women, thank you.*

*To all the young girls considering a career in tech
and STEM, we need you, it is worth it and you can do it!
Keep pushing forward, even if you are the only girl in the class.*

*For every woman who is working each day
to make her mark in this world, we all benefit
from your accomplishments, keep striving.*

TABLE OF CONTENTS

PROLOGUE

Making Your Desires Known

C andace Benson, a woman in tech and founder of Camp Tech, recently made this statement when talking about having a professional vision: *"Don't talk about it...BE about it."* How does her statement resonate with you? To me, it is about making our ideas, desires and areas of interest a focus each day.

It's about recognizing that the work you select, commitments you agree to, networking you make time for, sponsors you identify and words you choose to describe your value and future goals pave a noticeable path.

I did not realize early on in my career how the actions in my day would either align or misalign me with my future goals. I now realize I was not alone. Many women navigate the workforce without a career map.

This book, filled with action-based strategies, was created to share proven advice to catapult you toward your professional goals. Of course, I am not expecting you to address or even embrace all these strategies at once. I am suggesting that you take a few throughout the book that resonate with you now to explore, define and incorporate into your schedule. Over time, I encourage you to revisit this book and integrate additional strategies into your week.

By leveraging many of these strategies, more opportunities will come into play around your identified areas of influence and impact. It is important to note that through many of my interviews, keynotes and discussions with professional women through the years, I have learned to move away from focusing on landing specific titles. Instead, I encourage professionals to strive for amplified levels of *influence* and *impact*—two words you will see referenced throughout this book.

PREVIEW TO WHAT IS AHEAD

My aspiration for this book is to encourage you to identify ways to maneuver a professional path that maximizes your talents. Some of the strategies in this book that are based on research might leave you feeling like you are swimming upstream—at least initially—but I encourage you to stretch in new directions.

My goal within each chapter is to provide a playbook specifically for professional women to make professional goals a reality. Hopefully, it serves as motivation to help you seek out what you are looking for and to go after it.

I have integrated more than 100 articles and 20 exercises to capture your current state and future desired areas of influence and impact. To give you a taste of what is ahead, here are some examples of the content I've included in this book.

Dr. Travis Bradberry, an American author who writes on the subject of emotional intelligence posted the "9 Habits of Profoundly Influential People" on LinkedIn. I can relate to many of Bradberry's habits, but one habit really resonated with me:

> ***Influential Leaders Are Proactive***
> *Influential people don't wait for things like new ideas and new technologies to find them; they seek those things out.*

I love the idea of pursuing a dream, an idea, a new role or new initiative, especially when you are not 100 percent ready or prepared to embrace what is possible. I will talk about the **benefits of stretch projects and building your risk muscle**. This book also includes specifics about **facilitating strategic conversations** with key decision-makers, **leveraging a sponsor** to align you with an influencer or applying for a new initiative. All of these proactive actions take a level of confidence and self-efficacy.

Self-efficacy has been defined as the extent or strength of one's belief in one's own ability to complete tasks and to reach goals. This can be seen as the ability to persist and a person's ability to succeed with a task.

Sure they can be scary requests and actions, but if you don't ask or apply, I can guarantee the answer is always going to be no! Honestly, outside of a possible few minutes of discomfort and possible embarrassment, what do you have to lose? **Making your**

desires known well before you are 100 percent prepared is critical to your professional growth because when you are 100 percent ready for the opportunity, it is likely that it has lost its sizzle. It no longer has the same types of challenge associated with it.

But be aware, it is not uncommon for women to wait to raise their hand for an opportunity or to ask permission to start something in fear of letting others down. Research shows genders assess job descriptions differently and often decide to apply or not apply for different reasons. Did you know most women apply for a job when they are 100 percent qualified based on the requirements of the job description, while men apply when they meet 60 percent of the qualifications? This finding is based on many research studies and appears in Tara Sophia Mohr's 2014 *Harvard Business Review* article titled "Why Women Don't Apply for Jobs Unless They're 100% Qualified."

Waiting until you're 100 percent ready can stifle most professional women. These days many job descriptions are longer than one page and often run two to three pages with line after line of requirements. You can likely see the correlation: The longer the job description and related requirements, the less likely it is that women will apply. In Mohr's article, a woman states that the most common reason for not applying is she "didn't think they would hire me since I didn't meet the qualifications, and I didn't want to waste my time and energy."

Self-induced boundaries have held many great women back from making a difference. John Bates, in his article "Women Say No," shares a story of an opportunity where 10 men and 10 women were asked to give TED Talks:

> *When TEDx organizers in the U.S. and Europe ask 10 men to speak, nine say "Yes." When TEDx organizers in the U.S. and Europe ask 10 women to speak...nine say "No." And, I understand there are myriad reasons for this. Even myriad good reasons for this, but here's the part I think we need to think about. When those nine women say no, they get to make NO DIFFERENCE.*

Now I know firsthand that women often have many demands for their time inside and outside of work. It could be that these professionals had competing factors. But think about Mohr's statement as it related more toward self-approval and not necessarily time. When you turn down an opportunity not because you are not interested or because you cannot do it, but because you think you are not ready, you could be turning it down for many people behind you. Saying "no" based on fear and all the negative associations of not feeling ready can cultivate undermining energy related to your capabilities and beliefs impacting your ability to progress naturally, which could have lasting impact on your professional path.

If we don't show up, stand up or speak up, then how will others know we are relevant, ready and able? Bates ends his article with encouraging words: "I know it's scary. I know you're not as much of an expert as you could conceivably be, I know that you have a lot of other things going on right now. Here's what I'd ask you: Is it important to you? If not, don't worry about it. It's not important. But, if it's important to you, really important, then be willing to say YES and make a difference."

Ahhh, just soak in his words for a moment—envision yourself with the influence and impact you desire. What does this look like and how does it make you feel? If you can embrace an image and feeling of your future desires you can likely achieve it.

Striving for opportunities and related roles with more influence and impact can be very rewarding. The "Women Want Five Things" executive summary written by The Center for Talent and Innovation's Sylvia Ann Hewlett and Melinda Marshall, illustrates that women in leadership positions have more impact and influence to push energy and activities toward things that matter. In fact, their finding may actually surprise you:

> *Women start their careers hungry to attain a powerful job, but lose their appetite as they age. Even for women without children, and those who are breadwinners, power loses its luster for the 35 to 50 age group. Women do not understand that power can give them what they want. They perceive the burdens of leadership outweighing the benefits when in fact power, our data reveals, is what allows women to thrive and flourish. In all geographies, women with power enjoy the ability to reach for meaning and purpose, to empower others, and be empowered far more than women without power expect. In the U.S. and UK, women with power are able to flourish far more than women without power expect.*

The Ability to...	Expectations	Reality
Flourish	18 percent	58 percent
Excel	70 percent	87 percent
Reach for Meaning and Purpose	26 percent	63 percent
Empower Others and Be Empowered	14 percent	61 percent

Source: Sylvia Ann Hewlett and Melinda Marshall. "Women Want Five Things." The Center for Talent and Innovation: Dec. 9, 2014.

Wanting to be more impactful and influential was my goal throughout my career. I was not always striving for titles, but I was stretching for new positions within well-managed teams that fostered diverse thinking and talent. I have been told numerous times in my career, to "stop pushing," "you are not ready," "you will never be able," all of which could have crushed my spirit and self-belief. But each time I was pushed down, I got back up. It might have taken a few months, but through positive self-talk, great mentors and sponsors, and passion for my ability to make a difference, I moved back to a position where I could regroup, re-evaluate and reposition myself for what was next.

My professional journey has not been easy—as you'll learn reading this book—and many steps took longer than I anticipated. But I took every hurdle and "No" as getting me one step closer to "Yes." I was honest with myself about my professional gaps. I built bridges where I could. I aligned with where I wanted to go by leveraging many of the strategies I share with you in this book. In fact, many of these strategies I have used numerous times in my career with tremendous results. Each has had its place, and I have embraced them at different times to change business units, publish books, start industry groups, share advice within notable media, start a business and be recognized by numerous organizations for my contribution to women and girls.

Over time with noticeable results, I have become more proactive—even when the first inquiry starts with "No," or the polite "Not now, we have someone else in mind" or "You do not have the right credentials." These undesired responses now do not seem to deter me.

Now, I am much more confident that I can figure most things out, even when I am only partially ready. Sure, I may fail or arrive at a different endpoint than expected, but I am confident I have the tools, connections and experience that will guide me along the way.

What I have learned throughout my career is that people don't fall into great positions, roles or opportunities. These opportunities come after you have stretched yourself to access the next level of your courage, risk-taking, perseverance and willingness to manifest what you desire. These decisions, actions and interactions create the momentum and acceleration to catapult you forward.

I hope this book inspires you to accelerate what you know is possible.

FILLING THE VOID

Before we get into the book, I'd like to share a little about my professional journey. Often, I am asked how and why I started Tech Savvy Women (TSW).

To be honest, it had been a soft, delicate voice that I heard in my thoughts from time to time over a three-year period telling me that this was something I should do. The timing, however, just never seemed right as I spent most days challenged to stay on top of my demanding job, young family and all my other competing to-dos.

Girls' nights out, unfortunately, were more of a luxury. After having two children in 19 months at the age of 35, while leading a territory with a multimillion-dollar quota, I realized I needed something that filled my bucket. I was eager to find more relevance and truth, so I made time to attend book clubs, church groups, home parties and other gatherings that brought women together. As I drove home from most of these meetings, I still felt that I was yearning for something else.

At the time, I was not sure what I was searching for in these groups. In retrospect, I was craving more meaningful conversations with women who could relate to my madness: organizational changes monthly, new quarterly objectives, customer outages, intense deadlines, buried biases, unexpected travel—and that was just at work. It didn't include all the things happening at home with two young children and a working spouse.

After many years, I brought that delicate voice to the forefront by socializing it with other women in the technology field. Although I had little time for another initiative, I put a stake in the ground and started a gathering with women who could relate and facilitate the conversation and support I craved.

Twelve delightful, awesome, authentic women attended our first event in August 2008. These women brought laughter, empathy and perspective—I provided great wine and food. Within this relatable conversation, we highlighted a few things we would like to see in the future as we all committed to meet again:

- Authentic conversation.
- Support for each other and our journeys.
- A break from the madness.
- Good wine.

The entire event cost just a few hundred dollars. As I drove home from that first event, I felt like I found a place where I could be myself, laugh louder than normal, share my fears and receive some great advice, support and guidance.

Over the years, TSW has evolved. Great women continue to show up online and in-person because the conversation is effective, the events are helpful to their careers and the wine is usually needed. With lots of buzz over the years, TSW has been featured in many magazines including *Forbes*, *Smart Business* and *CBC*. It also has been featured on many radio shows and blogs.

Throughout these years, many men in technology and related fields have contacted me to ask how to get involved, how to get access to these experienced women in tech or how to mentor these great women. All of these related conversations have parlayed into some interesting conversations, articles and executive roundtables where we discuss attraction and retention strategies and the benefits of thought-diverse teams and organizations.

It took me years to get the confidence to listen and acknowledge my inner voice, reprioritize my schedule and ask other women to join me for fear I would be wasting their time and mine. Today, the group is more than 2,500 experienced women within technology and related fields. Many of the women who participate in TSW are product creators, team leads, developers, marketing experts, experienced senior sales women in tech, professional service leads, support specialist, technology executives and entrepreneurs building businesses. These women are paving the way for the next generation of young women joining the workforce.

TSW would not be where it is today without all the fantastic women who come together for these events and exchanges in various cities and online. We plan to host meetings in strategic locations where we will continue to weave in great discussions, ways to accelerate your impact, great wine and unique experiences.

We initially leveraged LinkedIn to stay connected, share ideas and post jobs and events. We have evolved as our activities, events, videos and conversations continue to expand—in addition to our LinkedIn group, we host a YouTube Channel (www.TechSavvyWomen.TV) and a website (www.TechSavvyWomen.net).

I have met hundreds of amazing professional women along the way and created some lifelong friends. I have been invited to participate in fantastic events and gatherings based on the creation of TSW, but it is more than that. For me, it is about creating something that matters to others, which provides a safe place for women to come together, inquire, share and just be. We'll discuss this more in-depth in **Chapter 8: Finding Networking Groups that Work for You**.

TSW is not the first thing I built from scratch based on a gap. I have been known to start other initiatives along my career path that were on a smaller scale. Some of these initiatives were helpful, others were a lot of work, and some never amounted to much, but all have helped me prepare for this moment in time.

Know that not everything you do, build or participate in will be *the thing*, but know that it is all practice and lessons for where you need to go next. With that thought in mind: What have you been looking for? What continues to appear in your thoughts? Where do you desire to have more impact and influence next? Let's begin looking at how you can accelerate your impact on the world. It has become clear to me that there is rarely one event, one person or one action that catapults you in the direction of your life purpose; it is more often a series of decisions, actions and connections each day that creates the momentum for you to leap.

CHAPTER ONE

People, Network and Opportunities
+ How Ready is Your Network

W e're past the point of saying technology is becoming an integral part of our lives. It's happened, and the scope of that presence is likely going to grow. What has not seemed to change, even with the increased influx of technology, is that people—not machines, websites or apps—are the ones who make decisions related to our workforce. They are the ones who promote, fire, hire and support people. Those who have grown into leadership positions chart the course for those who aspire to one day become those leaders, or simply move up in the organization and take a larger role and responsibility in leading it.

The initial premise of this book was to act as a networking guide for professional women, but after many hours of conversations, research and experience, the scope has evolved to include strategic actions and areas of focus in addition to networking that will help manage your professional throttle. Many of these strategies I have leveraged to move into new positions, create additional relevance to expand my brand and open doors for the future. These strategies and insights are important because research shows great results in your current role do not guarantee a pathway to where you desire to go next. This is especially true for women, as demonstrated in the *Harvard Business Review* article "Women in the Workplace: A Research Roundup:"

> *A trio of researchers—Monica Biernat of the University of Kansas, consultant M.J. Tocci, and Joan Williams of the Hastings College of the Law—found this dynamic in*

> *their study of performance evaluations at a Wall Street law firm. The women received more positive comments (excellent! stellar! terrific!) than the men, but only 6 percent of the women (as opposed to 15 percent of the men) were mentioned as potential partner material.*

I am not suggesting that we all have the same desired end-state or that you are striving to be a partner, a top executive or industry leader. But recognizing there may be existing hurdles beyond the work for professional women, regardless of their desired end-state, requires a proactive plan.

Many will jump to the importance of networking, but I have found that while doing more networking without putting in the effort to make sure you're aligning with the right things can make you very busy, with no guaranteed momentum. Many professional women have contacted me months or even years after they have spent time networking and investing in the people around them only to find that their current reporting structure was hindering their next professional desire. I am not suggesting a one-size-fits-all, but I am suggesting you need to have a plan.

Through my work and related interaction with professional women, I have found that many professional women are relevant based on their current role. They often struggle, however, to effectively expand their scope of expertise and applicability based on where they desire to go next.

HOW READY IS YOUR NETWORK

In a recent *CIO* article titled "Great IT Leaders Must Be Great Connectors," Charles Araujo highlights the traits of successful people in the technology world. Araujo mentions many times the importance of your network, your connections and your ability to be a connector. These often have a direct correlation to your future path and related opportunities.

When you think about it, this is not specific to women in technology or even professionals within the technology field. Fostering and utilizing your network has value in all walks of life.

In a Careerbuilder.com article titled "Is getting a job really about who you know?" Anthony Balderrama asked job seekers, employers and experts to weigh in with their experiences on how they found their job. Among the many great insights, I especially like:

> *The last four jobs I've had I've gotten through some kind of networking—all four through different circumstances:*
>
> 1. *A friend inside the company served as a referral.*
> 2. *A friend inside the company put my resume at the top of a 300-plus resume pile by bypassing the recruiter and emailing it to the hiring manager directly (which she was able to see since she was internal and had the visibility).*
> 3. *A mentor at the previous job put me in touch with some of her connections, one of whom worked for a company that turned out to be looking for someone.*
> 4. *I cultivated a relationship with an industry peer/senior executive via email and Facebook over a year and a half. When she took a job as a managing director at a new firm, we met in person for the first time for lunch. Turned out, she was looking to build her practice group, and I was looking for new opportunities. It was synergistic. I'm currently in this position.*

As you can see, it is no surprise that networking and professional connections are an important part of your future trajectory.

With this much impact on your future potential, it is important to provide a professional guide that highlights not only the tools and techniques to enhance your networks and related connections, but also some of the other details that can help or dampen your professional growth. Many spectacular professional women have contacted me throughout their respective careers, giving me an interesting perspective to actions, activities and outcomes.

Based on these career conversations and related research, I created a keynote for professional women based on the reoccurring questions below that shaped the outline for this book:

- How do I increase my influence on my team?
- How do I get my ideas elevated to the right people?
- How do I prepare for the next professional progression within my company?
- Why do some people easily leap forward while others stay in the same position?

- How do I get the right people to know about my professional goals?
- Does LinkedIn matter to my career journey?
- How do I build an effective network that will pave the way for my future?

CHAPTER TWO

Gauging Your Relevance

How relevant are you for where you want to have more impact next? Does this seem like a silly question? At some level, I am sure you are thinking, "Well, I have been working in this field for more than 10 years, I would say I am relevant." But are you?

I ask this because it has been asked of me on different occasions and usually during different crossroads in my career. The question of relevance has often appeared when others may or may not know my experience, knowledge on a topic, initiative or my potential based on my results to date.

I specifically remember a time in my career when I thought many saw me as a key contributor and an obvious choice for that next promotion. But when I let others know I was ready for the next opportunity, I was politely asked to stay focused on my current role. When I did a bit more investigating, I was kindly told things such as: "Do you really think you are the most relevant for this new role?" "We, as a leadership team, just do not see you in the role you aspire to obtain next." And the best one: "There are others who are more experienced than you."

Well, I must admit, I did not think this feedback was deserved or appropriate, even if it had merit. At first, I was aggravated and angry that anyone would have the nerve to ask me such a question or imply that I was not qualified—or in their terms "not relevant"— for my desired next step. I could have benefited from Caroline Dowd-Higgins' advice in her 2015 post titled "When You Don't Get The Job: 4 Tips To Help You Bounce Back," where her first tip of four is: "Keep negative emotions in check." Looking back, I now see that my ego was bruised, and I was professionally frustrated that I could not move when I felt that I was ready. In fact, this is often a crossroads for many professionals.

With time, I found this topic of relevance to be insightful and meaningful as it related to my brand and my ability to accelerate in my desired direction. My brand and relevance are more important than I had imagined, especially to the people with the social capital critical in helping me pave my professional path.

For many, relevance becomes especially important as you move up in your career because there are often fewer roles to be promoted to and more people weigh in on who is ready, applicable, effective and interested and who is not.

As Pegine Echevarria states in a LinkedIn post titled "Mentally Tough Woman: An Ongoing Story:"

> *At any given moment, it is easy to give up and wimp out. At any given moment, there are tons of reasons, many rational and logical, to be soft, subservient, and self-sacrificing.*

Reading Echevarria's quote makes me reflect on that time. I now realize that I could have easily taken that "no, thanks" and turned it into an unproductive series of actions. But I recognized that I had high self-esteem and confidence in my abilities to achieve.

I thought self-esteem and confidence were similar—and I often interchanged them. After reading a book summary by Debra Stangl, one of my favorite women—founder of Soul Adventures in Sedona, Arizona, one of my favorite places in the world—I appreciated that they drive different actions.

Stangl provided a wonderful summary of the differences cited from *The Confidence Code*, written by Katty Kay and Claire Shipman:

> *When they started writing the book, Kay and Shipman used 'confidence' and 'self-esteem' interchangeably...they discovered that confidence is more action oriented, while self-esteem (which they refer to as a vitally important cousin of confidence) is more related to our emotional makeup. Self-esteem is all about how we feel about ourselves, as opposed to how we perform in the world. And, of course, if we don't feel good about ourselves, it's usually much more difficult to perform well in the world.*

As I read this, I could finally separate and associate with both terms separately and how they affect my mindset, decisions and self-talk.

After some extra glasses of wine and a few extra coaching sessions, I started down a professional soul-searching path that helped me better understand my professional gaps, which were preventing me from obtaining a global promotion I so desired at the time. I realized that I needed to be very honest with myself. I took some time to review the relevance of the candidate pool for the role I desired. It was professionally sobering to learn that the other candidates were more relevant than I was at the time for the role I desired. Think about this for a minute: How relevant are you to your customers, company and team? How relevant are you within your industry and peer groups? Now think about how relevant you are for where you are going next?

Beyond this experience, I have recently noticed a swirl of activity surfacing in conversations, executive direction and company missions around the theme **Be Relevant**.

I started asking people in my network: How relevant do you think you are for where you desire to have more influence and impact? I found through my informal survey that many professionals with more than 15 years in the workforce lean on years of experience, prestigious networks and situational career lessons to shape their relevance. But like many of us, they are now grappling with how to be more relevant as social media invades our inbox and shapes our brands.

With ongoing streams of data creating platforms, new influencers and competitors that continue to evolve, it is even more of a challenge to stay relevant.

Here are a few questions to prepare for new thoughts, actions and behaviors:

- What areas do I want to be more relevant in?
- Why do I need to be more relevant around this topic? (Topic can be replaced with product, industry, competitive landscape, etc.)
- Who needs to be aware of my flourishing knowledge and awareness in a particular area?

Once I have specific data on where I am looking to go next and why it is important for me to be more relevant in this particular area, I start researching people who are already there:

- Who is already relevant is this area?
- What title do they currently hold and for what company?
- What professional steps have they taken to get there?
- What groups do they belong to now?
- What have they posted, published or participated in within the last two years?
- What makes them uniquely equipped for the level of impact I desire next?

From these answers—many of which I find online—I make a list of people and their accomplishments and career milestones. I then identify similar activities in which I can work to increase my relevance. For example, obtaining a doctorate is not likely in my future. Writing articles and books, leading new initiatives, joining specific boards, expanding my network in new directors and being a keynote speaker at national and global conferences are all possible. Take a look at your notes from the above questions, and then make a list of what is possible for you.

The goal is to effectively create new behaviors that enhance your current work and align you to where you desire to go next. I know it does not sound easy, but if divided into daily activities it could be less than 30 minutes a day.

These new areas of focus and additional activities are often necessary when you are looking to advance your career, change teams or launch new endeavors.

Spend a minute thinking about these questions:
- Am I relevant based on where I want to accelerate my impact?
- Do the right people know about my accomplishments and related relevance?
- What activities can I incorporate into my week to increase my relevance?

Even though the initial answer to my request to move professionally forward was initially a "No, thank you," I later learned that "No, thank you" was more of a "Not now."

As I worked to increase my relevance, I dedicated a few hours each week through focused activities to increase my relevance in a specific area, which directly impacted my knowledge, self-esteem, confidence and network. I did this in a variety of ways. Many of my first steps related to engaging my network, finding events that align with where I was and where I wanted to go, and being prepared to share my accomplishments and desired next steps.

My actions were deliberate. After consistent effort and authentic actions, I was invited to some related conferences, executive strategy sessions, and eventually—around 10 months later—I was asked to interview for a similar position based on my enhanced relevance, relationships and experience. Many of the specific actions I took to enhance my relevance, engage my network, bundle my value and align with my sponsors are incorporated in future chapters.

CHAPTER THREE

Bundling Your Value

"So, tell me a little about yourself?" "What is it that you do?" These can be scary and sometimes intimidating questions—especially for a professional trying to make a good first impression.

Many immediately jump to their title and the company they work for, which may be an answer, but isn't likely a good representation of their business impact. Now if you are the CIO, CFO or CTO, this often speaks for itself, especially if you are working in a known company. But only a handful of women hold these or similar positions.

Many of us struggle with an advantageous response that showcases our impact and value since many of us do a variety of things each day, week and month, making it difficult to sum up in one title or statement.

In fact, many dynamic women I know are program managers, service specialists, developers, enterprise sales managers, marketing experts, entrepreneurs, regional leaders, product specialists, global leaders, technical engineers and partner managers. In addition to these titles, these same women are also house managers, community liaisons, troop leaders, adjunct professors, product developers, carpool drivers, fundraisers, financial advisers, yoga instructors and board members. The list goes on and on.

Many professional women are multifaceted and delivering at work and at home. Many have a subset of roles and responsibilities in each area of their lives. The responsibilities and impact per company, industry, community and household often vary. So stating your name and role may not directly correlate to your ability and accomplishments.

The standard answer or some form of: "I am Jane, and I work as a XXX at XXX" is likely to leave out your other levels of impact that could be, but are not limited to committees, nonprofit work and community initiatives.

Your answer to these common questions asked by others to understand who you are is an extremely critical piece to your professional equation. In fact, in Glenn Llopis' 2014 *Forbes* article "5 Common Career Regrets To Avoid," he mentions great points that parlay right into the idea of creating a distinction and defining personal brand. I encourage you to read this article since Llopis' key points play right into the importance of your professional positioning.

Although this seems like another thing to think about and strategize on, the good news is that you can leverage these types of inquiries as an opportunity to share where you are in your career, but more importantly where you are going.

Something to keep in mind as you are thinking about your response is "women are judged on their actual performance," which is important to know as you are crafting these responses. This was based on a Wall Street analyst highlighted in Vivian Giang's 2015 *Fast Company* article "The Surprising Ways That Networking Fails Women."

Now, knowing this key insight, when someone asks you about your work, it is vital to share a snapshot of your accomplishments while integrating your future aspirations. Some call this an elevator speech. Others call it a value statement. But before we get to the many articles and best practices, here are some questions to ask:

- What are your most important projects in the last five to seven years?
- What significant accomplishments have you achieved during this time?
- What special projects were you assigned?
- Why do you think you were assigned to these projects?
- What obstacles were you able to overcome during these projects?
- What where the known milestones or related metrics in which you were measured?
- What kind of recognition did you receive?
- Who could you call on as a reference or sponsor?

I often ask female-based audiences to think about these questions. Many women gloss over their accomplishments. In doing such, they do not describe themselves and their work with the detail many are looking for when making decisions on new hires, potential candidates and future board members.

An article by Minda Zetlin published in 2015 titled "12 Ways Women Unknowingly Sabotage Their Success" highlights the work of Wendy Capland, CEO of Vision Quest Consulting and author of *Your Next Bold Move for Women.*

> *There are many ways women work against their own odds of success. Capland says there are 12 eye-opening things women need to stop doing ASAP—from using minimizing language to failing to build a brand.*

Now, I'm not saying that it's easy to adjust an expression of yourself, but I'm hoping you will recognize where your responses are now and what you need to work toward as you continue to network in new ways.

Since it is difficult to capture and share a live interactive dialogue between two people getting to know each other, especially where a woman is describing her work, I think "The resume gap: Are different gender styles contributing to tech's dismal diversity?" by Kieran Snyder in *Fortune* might give some insight on how women and men differ when describing their accomplishments.

A few of the findings in the article by Snyder echo why the questions above are a good start to reformat your professional statement that answers the question: "What is it that you do?"

One of the first highlighted findings states: "Women's resumes are longer, but shorter on details than men." And is followed up with these additional details:

> *Yet when it comes to providing detail about previous jobs, the men present far more specific content than the women do. Everyone's resumes include their former job titles, but women are significantly more likely to summarize their prior work at a high level rather than describing their roles in detail. Ninety-one percent of the men include bulleted verb statements that describe their achievements on the job, but only 36 percent of women do.*

Snyder also notes the differences of how men and women show up in a resume. Now I am not assuming we all show up the same way in a resume as we do in a conversation, but I do think it gives us something to think about as we describe our previous roles and related accomplishments.

Surprised? I was. I know I've added to this problem over the years, and once I recognized it through these studies and articles, I worked to integrate more details and specific accomplishments within my online profiles and accomplishments.

One big area of improvement for me was recognizing when to use the phrases "us," "team" and "I." Many of us suffer from too much "us," "we" and "my team." Now there is nothing wrong with being a team player. Creating opportunities to compliment and showcase the work of your team often gets noticed, but there are also appropriate times to highlight your specific accomplishments, contributions and credentials.

In fact, there are many times when people are looking to understand who you are and how they can help you pave the way toward increased influence and impact.

In these instances, it is especially important that you are prepared with measurable and identifiable ways to showcase you.

So what is it that you do?

It is essential that you are able to effectively articulate in just a few sentences the value you provide today (current impact) based on measurement data points (accomplishments) and where you plan to drive results next (future aspirations). Why? Because people are listening for where they can relate, connect and help you.

Accomplishments + Current Impact + Future Aspirations

Now that you have a list of your accomplishments and notable professional experiences, you can start to craft a few sentences to share with other professionals in order to make new connections, find a mentor or sponsor, become aware of new opportunities and gather additional data.

Some professionals have more than one type of expertise or area of focus, so they often have a few different types of answers for these exchanges. For example, Amy is an experienced CFO at a nonprofit school for developers, the board chair of the local animal rescue and the alumnae chair for her undergrad college. It is likely her answer when asked "What do you do?" varies based on who she is talking to, what her aspirations are with this person and what type of event or person connected them, along with other variables.

There is no need to have multiple answers right now, but this might make sense for you in the future. For now, it is important to have at least one applicable answer to "What do you do?" or some version of this question. As you find comfort in sharing your accomplishments, current impact and future aspirations, you may find you need to create a few responses based on the different roles and responsibilities you currently hold and where you desire to accelerate your impact and influence.

If you need additional guidance, see **Appendix A** for a list of articles that may help you write your own elevator pitch or brand statement. In addition to these articles, you can always search online for value statements, and mission statements.

I try to follow my own advice because I sometimes make it much more difficult than it needs to be, especially when the real goal is to share information while making it easy for the other person to refer, connect or sponsor me.

If all else fails you can complete this simple statement:

I help _____ advance _____(a verb)_____ for/to _____.
I am looking to get involved in _____
and need help with _____.

Here's an example: *I help Company X sell their technology-based surgery products into new markets to minimize surgery recovery time and increase product sales. I am looking to get involved in a technology medical startup that can leverage my operational skills and need help with meeting someone that funds medical startups in this area.*

This example is one of many options, but you can see how it is short, relatable and has an ask based on the desired next step. This is yet another example of how to answer "What do you do?" I encourage you to find one that is authentic for you and provides a meaningful framework that highlights your accomplishments and invites others to help orchestrate connections and opportunities.

As many professionals echo at the end of any gathering or event, you may only come away with a few meaningful contacts and a fewer number of people who can help you connect the dots. Keep in mind, however, that it is not a contest. Building your network in a meaningful and authentic way takes time. In fact, I often suggest that women start looking for the right connections 12 months before they are truly interested in accelerating in new ways. This timeline can apply to a board seat, a new initiative or taking an existing role in new directions to increase impact.

After all gatherings and events, I follow up with my new connections. Sometimes I send email follow-ups first, but more often I send a personalized LinkedIn invitation first. I like this approach because it gives new contacts the ability to see my professional timeline, roles, milestone and network. Once they accept my connection, I have been known to follow up with email, especially if I need to send them specific data or files.

Follow-up is obviously the place where many fall short, so schedule time in your calendar to close the loop on new connections. If fact, as I add the event into my schedule, I also schedule 30 minutes the day after the event to send thank-you notes, LinkedIn invites and follow-ups.

I look forward to hearing how you leverage these pearls of insight as you strive for your future professional milestones. Be bold; share what you have accomplished, what you are working on now and where you plan to go next!

CHAPTER FOUR

Boosting Your Self-Efficacy

Now some of you may be ready to jump in, but for many, including me, there is sometimes a voice or feeling that overcomes us and fills our heads with the thoughts that this is not possible, and we are in way over our heads.

You are not alone. Bernard Marr, a best-selling business author, talks in a 2015 LinkedIn post titled "The 7 Biggest Excuses That Stop You Succeeding" about some common barriers that can stop many of us from preparing for what is next—time, money and self-esteem. There is an even bigger obstacle for many women—and men too—called **Self-Efficacy**.

As defined by Wikipedia, self-efficacy is:

> *The extent or strength of one's belief in one's own ability to complete tasks and reach goals. This can be seen as the ability to persist and a person's ability to succeed with a task. As an example, self-efficacy directly relates to how long someone will stick to a workout regimen or a diet. High and low self-efficacy determine whether or not someone will choose to take on a challenging task or 'write it off' as impossible.*

In the article "The Three Pillars of Leadership Confidence & How to Build Them," author Marissa Levin talks more about the combination of these two self-awareness elements:

> *When working with my clients, my goal is to develop them in a healthy combination of high self-esteem and high self-efficacy. This empowers them to confidently communicate their value proposition, and deliver on their brand promise.*

> *Many times, clients come to me with insecurity about their leadership abilities, or an insecurity/unawareness about their value in the workplace. Sometimes, it's both. As I tell my clients, we can't expect our clients to value us and have confidence in us if we don't see it in ourselves first.*

I find Levin's advice to be very valuable as it sheds light on a hurdle for many of us.

Levin's chart, below, "diagrams what happens when these two characteristics are imbalanced. The upper left quadrant, however, shows what happens when they are balanced."

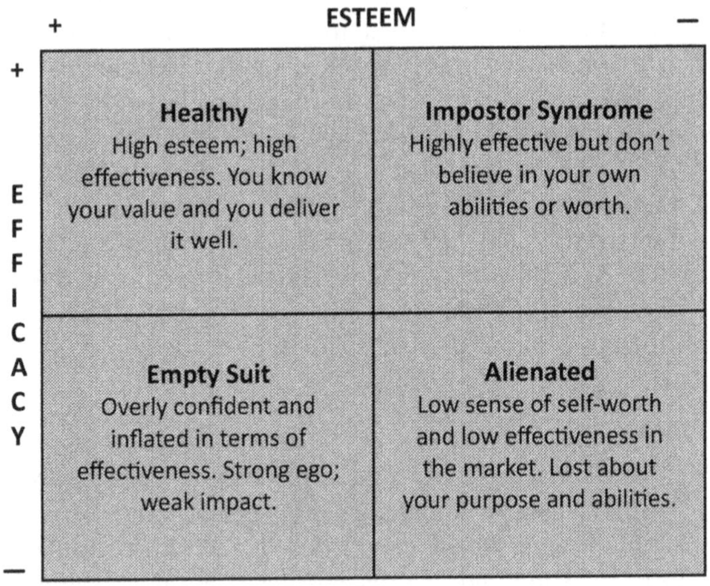

	ESTEEM	
Healthy High esteem; high effectiveness. You know your value and you deliver it well.	**Impostor Syndrome** Highly effective but don't believe in your own abilities or worth.
Empty Suit Overly confident and inflated in terms of effectiveness. Strong ego; weak impact.	**Alienated** Low sense of self-worth and low effectiveness in the market. Lost about your purpose and abilities.

(EFFICACY on vertical axis, + at top, − at bottom; ESTEEM on horizontal axis, + at left, − at right)

Source: Marissa Levin. "The Three Pillars of Leadership Confidence & How to Build Them." LinkedIn: April 5, 2015.

I am sure you know people from both genders that fit in all four quadrants. I have even found myself hopping between Healthy and Impostor Syndrome in the same day as I shift between projects based on my experience, knowledge and others who are involved. To keep this in check, I often ask myself "How am I feeling right now about the work I am doing?" When I get a new project I'm unsure about, I ask myself "Why are you feeling uncertain?" I spend more time acknowledging my thoughts and fears, helping me move back into confidence, mental strength and a comfort level of self-efficacy.

Sometimes to do this, I need to step away from my desk, take a walk, get a tea or talk to a sponsor to get some external momentum to move my mind and inner voice in a positive and healthy direction.

The Impostor Syndrome quadrant can have a strong hold on many professional women. Even though many work hard, and accomplish much, this Impostor Syndrome can make many not value their contributions. It is often the source for making us feel like we need to be 120 percent prepared and qualified before applying or nominating ourselves for any one position. For many in this top right quadrant, even if you achieve a new level of impact such as a new role or opportunity, you can find yourself questioning if you really belong.

I do not want you to think only certain people suffer from Impostor Syndrome. I have had many such spells throughout my career. I was surprised to learn that some of the most effective and accomplished women—and men—can feel unprepared and question their abilities, especially as new opportunities present themselves.

Jenna Goudreau wrote a great piece in *Fortune* called "When Women Feel Like Frauds They Fuel Their Own Failures," where she says:

> *Tina Fey once confessed that she sometimes screams inside her head, 'I'm a fraud! They're on to me!' Sheryl Sandberg attended a Harvard University speech called 'Feeling Like a Fraud' and decided they were speaking directly to her—she'd fooled them all. Sonia Sotomayor was 'too embarrassed' to ask questions while at Princeton University, and said, 'I am always looking over my shoulder wondering if I measure up.' Meryl Streep gets cold feet before every new project and told a reporter in 2002, 'I don't know how to act anyway, so why am I doing this?' Despite being plagued by self-doubt, which seems to have a place in all of us, these women barreled through it to the highest peaks of success.*

The Impostor Syndrome, which is now referred to as the Impostor Phenomenon (IP) was discovered by psychologists Pauline Clance and Suzanne Imes in 1978. According to a longtime lecturer on the phenomenon, Valerie Young, Ed.D., "Little has changed in the last three decades—except that more women than ever are susceptible."

Mike San Román offers tips for overcoming Impostor Syndrome in his *Fast Company* article "8 Practical Steps to Getting Over Your Impostor Syndrome:"

1. *Recognize that it exists.*
2. *When you receive positive feedback, embrace it with objectivity and internalize it. By denying it, you are hurting that person's judgment.*
3. *Don't attribute your successes to luck.*
4. *Don't talk about your abilities or successes with words like 'merely,' 'only,' 'simply,' etc.*
5. *Keep a journal. Writing your successes and failures down gives you a retrospective insight about them, and rereading them makes you remember equally both of them.*
6. *Recognize that the perfect performer doesn't exist and that problems will pop up eventually. Take them as little fires under you that make you move forward.*
7. *Be proud of being humble.*
8. *Remember that it's okay to seek help from others and that even the best do it.*

When I raised my hand for the promotion I previously mentioned, I had no idea all these obstacles existed both internally and externally. Although I have experienced many of these internal and external obstacles firsthand at various times in my career, I have recently learned about these formal terms and related research.

As I spend more time with executives interested in attracting, retaining and growing their diverse leadership teams, we find ourselves discussing many aspects of confidence, relevance, internal beliefs, self-efficacy, management styles and career paths for women. These studies, articles and related conversations have created more clarity for leaders, as we work together to effectively engage women at all levels of an organization while being mindful of why women stay, advance or sadly leave the corporate world.

It seems appropriate to end this section with these questions:
• Can I categorize my main projects and my related quadrants as they would fall in Levin's chart?

46

- What tools have I used to move toward the Healthy quadrant with high self-efficacy and value?
- When I think about where I desire to have more influence and impact, do I believe I can get there?
- What self-beliefs may be holding me back?
- What people in my network can help me foster more positive and effective self-value in my work?
- What have I learned from this chapter?

CHAPTER FIVE

Compiling Your Connections and Accomplishments

As I reflect on my professional choices since joining the IT industry in 1995 as a full-time IP network analyst, I now realize there was much more to my day than my work. There were many things I needed to know to open doors and continue to professionally advance that I surely did not acquire in the lecture halls.

What I have learned over the last two decades is that my connections, attitude, relevance, managers, mentors, sponsors and advisory boards are as important to my professional growth as the results I deliver independently or with and within my teams.

Before we jump into the various aspects of my career journey that accelerated my impact, it is often important to think about where you are now. Creating a starting point is necessary to determine how to maneuver the landscape.

I carefully selected the word compiling for the title of this chapter, as it reminds me of the hours of code I muddled through that opened doors along the way. I have had my fair share of mistakes both in life and in my code.

Luckily, a professional journey is assembled by a series of minutes, people, actions and outputs—innocently swapping the letter "o" with the numeral "0" usually will not turn all your work upside down. Unless, of course, you are coding and one simple misstep can create thousands of compiling errors. As I look at my career—yes, coding errors were painful—what often kept me immobile was not showcasing my work, leveraging my networks or having defined areas of focus.

Let's take a moment to think about the work you do today, how you show up and who is supporting you. Take a sheet of paper and write your answers to the following questions:

- What are the characteristics of my environment today?
- What work am I responsible for each day/month/quarter?
- Describe my direct manager? (supportive, undermining, hands-off)
- What is my attitude at work? Does it change throughout the day?
- Am I able to effectively manage change and uncertainty?
- Do people have to emotionally support me or do I emotionally support others?
- Who is currently aware of my work, outcomes, ideas and impact?
- What people would give me a glowing recommendation based on our work together?
- How much time am I taking each month to cultivate my network?

It is important to be honest with where you are starting as you work through each section of this book. Not everyone is great at building and nurturing their network, showcasing their outcomes or articulating their goals and professional requests.

In fact, I find many people in tech and related fields—both men and women—can be more introverted and spend little time on activities that can cultivate the right acknowledgment, opportunities and conversations. Many of these same professionals focus the majority of their day on getting work done, which is excellent for the team, project and company, but does not always create the same desired individual results as one might hope.

PROFESSIONAL CONNECTIONS AND ACCOMPLISHMENTS

Making connections and investing in your network is a lifelong exercise that can be intimidating, but is an important aspect to professional growth. You never really know which relationship might help you land that next project, promotion or opportunity.

There are many ways to foster relationships. Some feel comfortable with a more traditional approach of meeting in-person for a beverage or meal, while others embrace virtual meetings, conference calls, hangouts and online platforms.

As our work environments change with remote workers, contractors and multiple offices and locations, so has the way we work to build and foster relationships. With the help of social media and other online tools, more people in a variety of positions and levels are accessible, which was not the case years ago.

Here are a few questions to ask yourself in regards to the efforts you have made to build up your network:

- How do I foster new connections?
- Who have I invited to an introduction meeting outside my existing connections?
- Have I taken the time to update my online profiles?

Although some might not agree that dedicated time each day is necessary to foster your network, many find it to be a key part of their weekly schedules. Some professionals make phone calls, others meet for coffee or lunch, and some share articles, send emails or engage online.

When Cindy, a developer and team lead, aspired to join the board of directors for a local nonprofit to gain additional leadership skills and expand her network, she turned to her existing network. She could do this because six months before deciding on this direction, she spent 10 to 15 minutes each day on her LinkedIn profile ensuring it was up-to-date. In addition to these activities, she leveraged this and other online profiles to establish and maintain relationships that she might not interact with on a regular basis.

When she was ready to take on additional responsibility, it was her network that jumped in to make the initial connections. These warm introductions from people who already knew Cindy led to several meetings with the nonprofit's leaders and eventually some of its existing board members.

Cindy, of course, needed to take the lead after these initial connections, but it was her existing relationships that set up these first few meetings with the right people. From there, Cindy worked to learn more about the responsibilities and expectations, as well as share her accomplishments, desires and potential impact if she was given the opportunity to join the board.

It is important to note that Cindy did take the time to do research about the existing board members, reviewed the annual reports and investigated similar nonprofits to warrant her relevance and knowledge.

Note, your existing connections can be great at connecting you to key influencers or decision-makers, but it is up to you to do your homework so you are prepared for the conversation. In these introduction meetings, you will need to be ready to share why you are a great fit or an ideal candidate or the right person for the opportunity.

Be sure to have some strong professional statements ready that showcase how your attention and effort have made a difference to ensure others that you can bring value to the role.

Experience has taught me that women are not as likely to take the credit they deserve for what they have accomplished or individually contributed to a team or project. In fact, many play off their career milestones as "the team," "the opportunity" and even "the company culture," which can all have merit and impact to the outcome, but may not get you the recognition needed.

The "I" in your conversations is often important, especially when others are looking to understand your direct impact. Owning your accomplishments and being able to effectively articulate what you can accomplish is very important as you position yourself for the future.

Cathie Ericson, in a Glasshammer.com article titled "Voice of Experience: Alaina Percival, CEO, Women Who Code," states: "When you see someone doing a great job, applaud her." Percival advises:

> It's more difficult for women to talk about their career successes, but if you don't, no one will know to 'sponsor' you, ask you to speak at their conference or invite you to be on their board. Being able to publicly discuss your career success is crucial to advancement.

"Female workers are urged to champion their skill sets," states a 2015 The Telegraph (UK) article titled "Women needed in STEM jobs for the sake of innovation." "To some extent, self-confidence can be taught. Self-belief can be more complex."

The same article goes on to share Rachel Cook's story. Cook was an associate director at the engineering giant Atkins, which she joined as a graduate trainee in 1997:

> *I was afraid of failure, and felt I had to 'tick all the boxes' before I was confident enough to progress. When I finally applied for my last promotion, people said I should have done it years ago.*

In the same article, Ann Watson, CEO of Semta, says:

> *Women need to showcase what they have achieved, taking the credit rather than being too modest. Setting career goals is also a big problem—perhaps one reason why fewer women make it into the boardroom—so this is a major focus of the career development that Semta is currently delivering.*

What thoughts have these examples generated for you?

Let's jump back to Cindy's journey. During some additional meetings with key decision-makers, it was necessary for Cindy to present her accomplishments, goals, interests and potential value as a future board member. After a four-month courting period, Cindy was invited to join the board when a board member's term ended. The offer to join the board was not immediate, but Cindy was assured that she was in line for the next board seat.

If you too are interested in joining a nonprofit board, visit www.TechSavvyWomen.TV to view three interviews with Elizabeth Hosler Voudouris, who at the time of recording was the executive vice president of Business Volunteer Unlimited, a national organization that has trained and matched more than 2,100 business executives and professionals on the boards of more than 450 nonprofits. Voudouris highlighted some of the leadership benefits professional women can acquire when joining nonprofit boards.

Cindy's experience is just one example of a professional woman who set her sights on a desired area of impact and some of the steps she took to accelerate her path. There are many paths from where you are now to where you desire to be, and it is likely that your professional aspirations will evolve over time.

Regardless of where you desire to go or how you plan to pave your path, my experience and research shows that taking the time to assemble and enhance your professional connections now while being able to articulate your value through your professional brand could create meaningful opportunities and connections later.

CHAPTER SIX

Enhancing Your Professional Brand

What is your professional brand? Is it your title, your last project, your community work, your network or a combination? I've learned that my brand evolves and is often a combination of what I have aligned with in the past and the things I focus on each week.

I did not realize how important professional branding—defined by your accomplishments, current impact and relevances based on your future aspirations—was in my career journey until I was told, "No, you cannot apply." Recognizing my professional aspirations did not align with how people perceived me was a big eye-opener. At first, I did not think I had the ability to change it, but now I know with focused effort, professional brand can and should evolve.

As you are looking to accelerate your impact, it is important to identify, investigate and, when you can, oversee what defines your professional brand. Your brand has likely helped you land in the role you have today. But ask yourself: Will it open doors for the areas you hope to accelerate tomorrow?

In my experience, people learn and make assumptions about you based on your interactions, deliverables and online activities. You obviously cannot control all aspects of your brand, but I have found you can often select work and activities to shape it in your desired direction.

If you are unsure of your current professional brand, make an effort to inquire, gather and assess where your brand sits today. In addition to asking some close professional friends, you can collect information during annual reviews, through feedback from customers and you can even hire a professional coach to gather opinions from a defined list of professionals. Some companies offer

360 reviews, and some leaders encourage informal feedback and offer other avenues for undisclosed anonymous feedback.

All these sources of information, at some time, can help you collect the insight you need to understand how others perceive you. These data points are essential and can act as indicators of your brand that can vary widely among people, groups, companies and connections, but can extract some common themes.

The goal of the gathering exercises in this chapter is to understand where you are starting from now, so you identify your gaps to work toward the professional brand you desire. It may seem overwhelming, but you can tighten, evolve and even enhance your professional brand as you focus on new activities, engagements, participation, people and sponsorship.

Lois Frankel, author of *Nice Girls Don't Get the Corner Office*, aligns with the advice I often share with professional women in a Women for Hire interview:

> *Consciously build your brand. We are all brands in the workplace. We have to differentiate our brand from all the others, hone it, market it and get regular feedback about it. Write down what you want people to say about you when you leave a room. Then attach specific behaviors to each of these words so that you act in ways that enable people to see you as you want them to. If you want people to say, 'She really knows her stuff' then you'd better show up to every meeting armed with data, keep up with trends in your field and share them with colleagues, and speak up in meetings.*

For many, your professional brand often aligns with where you have been and often not where you want to have momentum and impact next. Think again about your resume and online profiles. Do these overviews primarily showcase where you have been in your career journey? If so, that's a great starting point.

Think of yourself as a website for a moment: If people wanted to find you for a new opportunity, board seat or community initiative based on where you desire to have more impact, what would they type in Google? What would they search for on LinkedIn?

Now, think about your online professional profiles and online activities. Would you show up in their search results? If so, would you appear as a viable option, someone they would want to talk with? To brand yourself for the future, you must find time each week to integrate new information, new connections and new discussions to increase your relevance based on where you desire to have more influence and impact.

You might think: When do I have time? How do I even start? In my experience, there are often opportunities all around you—at work, in your community and within social media platforms. Many of these spheres offer situations and provide opportunities for networking, knowledge and connections that could likely act as a stimulus for your brand.

Before you jump in, take some time to make a plan. Here are a few questions to help you narrow your efforts and focus your energy to enhance your professional brand:

Define Your Is: Where do you desire to have more influence or impact in the next 24 months?

Find Others: Where can I find others already creating this influence or impact?

Make Time to Research: Schedule time in your calendar each week to review the people you have found that are already aligned with similar roles or are making the impact you are looking to make next.

Schedule a recurring time in your calendar: Day____ Hour _____. The thing I like about scheduling it on my calendar is that I cannot dismiss it until I complete the task, so even if it is not exactly at the desired time, it eventually happens that day.

Locate Examples: Find example inquiries, requests or job descriptions as examples of where you desire to have more impact. Print these examples. Take time to identify commonalities, terms, connections, associations, linear links and integration opportunities.

Prioritize Your Actions: Determine actions you can take to close the gap between where you are today and where you desire to have more impact tomorrow. Make a list of professional activities based on your research. Some examples could be:
- Attend a conference.
- Submit a presentation for a call for papers.
- Connect with a few industry writers.
- Take a class or get certified.
- Join a new group, organization and/or initiative.

- Establish a relationship with an industry expert.
- Take on new projects at work.
- Self-nominate yourself for a specific project or initiative.

Your list will be determined by your goals, your research, what has worked for others and what you can reasonably and credibly accomplish. Don't be surprised if it takes some time. Expect to encounter some roadblocks along the way.

To receive new invitations you usually have to show up in the marketplace the way it expects to see you. You often have to participate in new activities, align with new industry terminology and package your related work as expected to complement your existing actions and accomplishments.

Get Feedback: Ask trusted sources to review your plan and to suggest additions to your action list. Be sure you are asking people who are truly interested in supporting your desire for growth.

I have had a few unfortunate opportunities where I have trusted some people who indirectly or directly worked to sabotage my efforts. In *The Working Woman's GPS*, I created a chart that helped me identify people who positively supported my current and future efforts, which has been extremely helpful throughout my life.

For the sake of this chapter, we simplified it to just a few columns:

Person or Description	Supports My Current Work & Contributions	Supports Me as I Stretch to Accelerate My Impact
John, Manager	+	+
Cheryl, Business Partner	/	—
Tom, Service Manager	+	—

(+) Yes, this person supports me.
(/) Maybe, this person supports me some of the time or I am unsure and have to be more mindful to determine if it is a + or —.
(—) No, this person does not encourage or support me.

It is important to build a trusted sphere of influence, especially during times in your life when you are looking to stretch in new directions. As a working woman, I know it takes a team of people to support my professional decisions, and I am aware of who and who does not want me to take on more or move more toward my desired goals.

Over the years I have had to make two types of adjustments:

- My trust sphere of influence. I have a circle of people, my advisory board, that have been with me for years and I truly cherish their ongoing love, support and reciprocation. As I have evolved, so have many of the people around me.
- My exchange of energy. I am now, more than ever, aware of the energy I exchange with people during conversations, online and in groups. I have learned to realize that my brand is all around me. I strive to consciously attract the energy I desire through my work, exchanges and actions.

I had to make some lifestyle changes to increase my positive energy. There was a time when my negative and self-destructive energies trumped my positive energy. There was a direct correlation to how I felt about myself, the people around me and the projects I took on.

If you are struggling with unproductive energy, I suggest you read my last book *The Working Woman's GPS*. After writing that book, I have become more aware of my commitments and the people I attracted to my network, my choices and exchanges of energy.

Make Updates: Most plans need assessment and sometimes a sharpened focus as you increase your discoveries, and this likely will be no different. What I found when actively working to align my efforts toward a more technical level of impact is that I need to be sure people outside my trusted network are aware of my background, my new activities, knowledge and connections. Find opportunities to share your relevance with the people you know and the people you meet along the way. It will help you manifest opportunities that align with where you desire to have more impact.

Any and all of these intersections and connections could be critical to the acceleration of your path.

It is likely that these new people will research you or review your online profiles before contacting you or offering to meet you in person. Be sure your profile showcases relevance to your path with where you have been and where you are going next.

Ask for References: It is always great to have references before you need them. Today, online references can truly enhance your profile.

Online references quickly inform board members, recruiters and hiring managers as to how others perceive your work and impact.

As you likely know from being on the other side of this request, references need time—and some need guidance. One thing that has helped my references is that I only ask for one or two sentences. People often write more, but it minimizes the pressure, and most people can complete this request in just a few minutes. The other thing I do is offer to provide a short draft or a few keywords. Many find a few suggested ideas streamlines the results, often making it easier to get started.

I have pointed many to my online references to secure keynotes, consulting projects and new opportunities. It is something that can take extra time, but can be tremendously helpful, especially if you work to obtain them before you need them.

Read Often: Read current events within your desired field and share this information with groups, people and team members. Be selective and focused on your posts, related terms and themes. A quick way to categorize yourself online is to post on the same topic often. Your personal brand can benefit from SEO too. "SEO Tips For Building Your Personal Brand," by Kevin Gibbons is a great article filled with strategies to help advance your brand.

Join Online Groups: A wealth of information, experts and trends are concealed in online groups. Researching and joining relevant groups online to stay abreast of current topics and key players in your industry can be tremendously helpful.

When I was starting Tech Savvy Women in 2008, I joined as many relevant groups as possible to be sure I was not duplicating efforts while noting best practices and key leaders. Another time I leveraged a similar strategy was in 2011, when I was publishing my first book. I joined book related groups to navigate the publishing world to uncover my action items, potential potholes, industry experts and related opportunities.

As you can imagine, this did not all happen in one week or even one month. These steps took almost a year to completely crystallize. I suggest moving in this order to be sure you do not get over excited and jump into a bee's hive that could impact your brand negatively. These activities were necessary for me to reposition myself for a new position when I was initially told "No, you cannot apply for this internal move."

Now, if you are looking to engage more in your current discipline, and not necessarily looking to take on the work right now or move to a new position, this list summarizes the approach that has worked for me when working myself into new online groups:

- Join groups based on where you are and where you want to go.
- Research the members, posts, history and mission.
- Receive and read the posts—many platforms provide weekly digests.
- Support others—like posts that mean something to you or that you benefit from.
- Provide feedback or comment on posts (remember the flow of reciprocal energy).
- Find synergy with other group members and send them an invite to connect.
- Post relevant information based on your research and associated posts.

Participate in group conversations with relevant comments and posts. It can impact your SEO rankings and your online brand. Think back to where you want to increase your impact and align your posts and activities to stretch in your desired directions. Posts with similar terms and focus can enable your online brand and relevant ranking within specific topics. Online groups were a key catalyst, positioning me in new ways for many of my professional goals and aspirations.

Be Open: Be open to new connections and groups. You never know which connection or group of people will catapult you toward your desired areas of impact. With the right amount of attention and focus, it is possible to enhance your professional brand. If you still have aspirations, yet don't know how you will find the time, this is not something you have to do alone. You can always get help or hire resources to get the process going and even participate online on your behalf.

The most important thing you can do is know where you are looking to accelerate your impact, who is already there and what gaps you need to fill to align your brand for what you aspire to do next.

After some time you should start to see indicators that your brand is evolving. Some clear indicators are:

- An upswing in requests for your time around your new conversations.
- A theme among new connections.

61

- An outreach from new teams or groups.
- An acknowledgment or reposting of your content.

Your future is now, how you show up matters, who you bring with you matters and where you focus your time matters. It all matters if you want to contribute in new ways.

It is your career. Don't leave your brand—a preview to what is possible—to chance.

For more on improving your personal brand, see **Appendix A** for a list of articles that may help.

CHAPTER SEVEN

Targeting Your Relevance to Enrich Your Brand

It is not uncommon to be overwhelmed at the thought of incorporating new activities into your day in order to increase your relevance and enrich your brand as you prepare for your next professional step. Although I was clear on what I wanted to do next, I was not initially sure what to do first after I was strongly advised not to pursue my next desired step.

I had some ideas of how to dissect the steps necessary to move from where I was to where I wanted to go based on the work in the last chapter, but I honestly did not initially know how fast and how diligent I should be in my existing role and within my industry. More importantly, I did not know where I was going to find the time. I was already so busy at work and at home that I could not imagine adding more things to my day, especially because I knew it would be cutting into things I had already committed to.

After spending more time looking online for other similar roles— not because I was looking to change companies, but because I wanted to understand the desired requirements—I decided to categorically investigate the professionals that were already working in a comparable role to the one I desired. Over a few weeks, I reviewed about 25 professional profiles of people who were making the professional impacts that inspired me.

In addition to this, I also printed out 10 relatively similar job descriptions for open positions which, looking back, became the starting point for my targeted action plan to increase my relevance based on where I desired to accelerate my impact.

If you are not as clear on what is next, but you do know you are ready to tackle new work, new initiatives and create new professional opportunities, here are some ideas to get laser focused on enriching your brand to increase your relevance to enhance conversations, create new connections and manifest new opportunities.

IDENTIFY POTENTIAL NICHES

With the vast amount of data each day, it is important to focus in on strategic areas within a specific industry, which will allow you to weed through and find the data that really matters to your professional path. Being a developer is an awesome career, but how about a developer focused in on a specific language within a specific industry and maybe even a specific area? For example, a Ruby on Rails developer in the finance industry that works specifically within online banking apps or an infrastructure engine that specializes in the data transfers between private and public clouds or a lawyer that works on mergers and acquisitions for the software industry or an executive that launches new consumer based products for a particular group of people.

I love Susan A. Friedmann's book *Riches in Niches: How to Make It Big in a Small Market*. It has encouraged many people, including me, to focus on one aspect of an offering or industry. The goal is to position myself as "an Expert in a Niche—a sweet spot known as a *nichepreneur*—the most surefire route to success." Her focus is geared toward entrepreneurs, but her message and best practices are practical and effective for any professional.

This idea of niching also rings true for professionals interested in future board seats. Tracy E. Houston, M.A., president of Board Resources Services LLC, includes similar advice in her recent e-book Becoming a Public Company Director. Houston's series of e-books are great resources for professionals looking to join boards of directors. When we spoke for our video "3 Key Strategies to Obtain a Board Seat," Houston mentioned:

> *Becoming an expert in a particular area within a specific industry often better positions you for future board seats.*

Now there may be some fear in picking a niche or area of expertise. Brennan Dunn gives some great tips in his 2015 post "Overcoming The Fear Of 'Choosing A Niche.'" Dunn's suggestions are geared to entrepreneurs since people do not often talk about niching in corporate settings. Most of Dunn's advice can be applied to the individual working on positioning him or herself for the marketplace and future advancements.

There are many tips I could highlight from Dunn's article, but the one that jumped off the page for me is: "You need to solve a worthy problem." You'll hear this from me as it relates to networking and again as we discuss market relevance. **Think of yourself as a problem-solver** and focus on an area you can best build your skills, expertise and network to create differentiation and marketability.

MAKING THE TIME

As many of us struggle with finding time, the "Power of No" chart has helped me clearly understand where I'm spending my time and if my choices align with my goals. I use this chart almost every week and have shared it with thousands of professionals since its creation.

THE 'POWER OF NO' CHART

Commitments	Requester	Alignment	Energy	Time	Remove

It helps me identify opportunities in my schedule that increase my relevance and impact. In many cases, it gives me permission to let go of some commitments that no longer align or belong on my calendar. The ability to stop doing something that is not adding value to my work or my life frees up time within my schedule to select more relevant activities. These two steps are important to excel in my current work and more importantly, increase my relevance to enrich my brand based on where I want to increase my impact:

1. What should stay in my calendar?
2. What should I remove to make room for more relevant commitments?

Many of the professionals I have shared this chart with are working through a variety of professional situations to maximize the use of their time and align their commitments to current deliverables and future desired goals.

At a high level, this chart is focused on commitments to which you have already said, "Yes, I will allocate time to these initiatives, tasks or people." This format helps me and many others quickly get an understanding of where we spend our time and if our commitments are aligned with where we naturally excel. It also provides an opportunity to create space in your schedule to integrate relevant commitments that will help position you for where you desire to have more impact and influence in the future.

HOW TO USE THE 'POWER OF NO' CHART

I have branded this chart "Power of No." I find most professionals are already overcommitted in their current areas of focus and most need increased relevance to open new doors and be invited to new opportunities. To create room in their schedules for what is ahead, they often have to say "no" to something that they already said "yes" to in order to move toward their desired areas of impact. This six-column chart provides professionals with a clear strategy to align with commitments that will create more momentum in their schedules to help them catapult forward.

Commitments: Make a list of your professional commitments. These are tasks, meetings, conversations and activities in which you're already committed to doing. This column should align with how and where you spend your time now. This column may take a few weeks to complete as you realize all the commitments you have each day, week and month. When I started this exercise, I made a weekly chart, a monthly chart, and a quarterly chart because not all of my tasks and commitments occur on a daily or even weekly basis. The goal is to understand what occupies your 168 hours each week.

Requester: Who asked you to work on this commitment? List the person who asked or requested you to take on each commitment by name. This requester could be you, a family member, boss, neighbor, community person or co-worker. The options are endless. I added this column after I initially built this chart and found that I had repeat requesters for my time that often resulted in the requestor's advancement and or enjoyment, not mine.

Alignment: Does this commitment effectively align with where you are now or where you plan to accelerate your impact? Use (Y) to indicate, "Yes, this commitment aligns with my goals." Use (N) to indicate, "No, this commitment does not align with my goals."

Energy: What kind of energy do you get from this commitment? Do you look forward to this commitment or do you dread this commitment? Use the symbols of plus and minus or a slash to describe how you feel about this commitment. A (+) means this commitment energizes you, a (−) means you don't look forward to this commitment and a (/) means you have mixed feelings about this commitment.

Time: How much time does this commitment require? Time is an important column because if a commitment only takes a few minutes or a few hours each week, it might not be as big of a drain as a commitment that takes several hours each week. Where possible, list the amount of time each commitment takes. Time should factor into your decision for the next column.

After you have taken the time to jot down your commitments and complete the related columns, are there any surprises? How many pluses (+) and minuses (−) do you have in your chart? It is often interesting because many people have more commitments than they imagined. Many people who leverage this chart say how surprised they are that several of their commitments do not align with their current or future goals. They are often even more surprised to learn that many of their "yeses" do not create positive energy, which tends to impact the level of energy they have each day.

Remove: As you complete this chart, examine each and every commitment you have listed. Are there some commitments that can be removed or cut back? Use Y to indicate that you can remove this commitment; use M to indicate that you may be able to remove this commitment. You can assume that the other commitments that are not marked in this column with a Y or an M are aligned with your goals and should continue to be a focus for you at this time.

There are many more insightful aspects of this chart. If you want more details on how to use this chart to create more relevant commitments, purchase the online video "Power of No" at **www.JJDiGeronimo.com/no**. In this 12-minute video, I share specific steps, strategies and examples along with the chart.

Things to Consider: If there are commitments in your chart and in your life that do not align, it is likely pulling everything in your day down. These commitments, with negative (−) energy, often take more time than you desire to give. This chart hopefully brings these misaligned commitments to the forefront. If possible, it is time to work on delegating, eliminating or outsourcing the commitments within these rows. It can take time to remove commitments, but knowing what no longer serves you is as important to creating your future actions. If you have a plus on alignment but a minus on energy, this is completely normal. It could be work you need to get done to get you where you want to go next, but you may not enjoy it. We all have had work we have to do to check a box or pave the way for our next set of goals. Sometimes you can get help on these items and other times you just have to push through them. If you have both a plus in alignment and energy, these commitments often align with your natural talents, and you usually shine when doing this work. The goal is to increase these commitments in your life so you are aligned with work that taps into your natural talents. These commitments might give you additional insight into where to go next with your career.

Now that you have spent some time looking at each row, it should be obvious which commitments need further investigation and can even potentially be removed from your life. I have seen many professionals align with commitments that have limited value for too long. This chart has been an eye-opener and trigger for many over the years. If you experience a new level of awareness or even a shocking discovery, please let me know. I get a real thrill from these notes and have collected many over the years after sharing this chart through my travels.

What I have learned is: Agreeing to the wrong requests for my time in the form of a commitment negatively influences the right requests and often impacts my ability to create my desired results.

LEVERAGE ONLINE PLATFORMS AND TOOLS

There are many ways to access new information and people to create additional value and relevance. It took me a few months to create space in my life and in my calendar. I was eager to add more relevant activities not only based on my current work, but also to help pave the path for future interest and initiatives.

I quickly realized that I needed more effort to create momentum. A few senior women ahead of me mentioned how important it is to find some additional resources to help with the existing workload and new endeavors. This was key for me to create the velocity I desired. I needed assistance on many aspects within my professional sphere. I was initially focused on building my online brand. I too benefited from engaging additional resources to help me get the work that seemed necessary based on the research highlighted in previous sections.

Like many, I subscribed to **Google Alerts** for years, which has helped my career path evolve. I recently started using **Backstitch** to help me personalize the web and filter data in real-time that directly influences my business activities. I have even invested in adjunct resources such as researchers, writers, personal assistants, and web and SEO experts. I have found these specific resources through my network and online. Some of the websites I have used to locate these resources are **Upwork** and **Fiverr** where you can hire talent the same day you post the project.

At different points in my career, I used different online resources. I have a wonderful group of professional consults—experts and industry-focused resources that I have worked with for years. We started small with just a few hours a week. Some of these working relationships have blossomed, and others were a point in time. I am still actively connected with many of the people I have hired over the years, and we often help connect each other to potential partnerships, customers and interesting opportunities. In addition to these fantastic people, I make a point to join specific online groups, especially as I am starting a project.

When I was working to publish my first book, *The Working Woman's GPS*, I joined many author and publishing groups on LinkedIn. The groups on LinkedIn have been enormously helpful in every phase of my career.

As the HootSuite Blog highlights in Donné Torr's article "The Benefits of LinkedIn Groups and LinkedIn Company Pages," LinkedIn Groups provide a place for professionals in the same industry or with similar interests to share content, find answers, post and view jobs, make business contacts and establish themselves as industry experts.

For weeks after joining these new groups within LinkedIn, I observed the conversation to gain an understanding of the publishing process, common conversations, pitfalls, best practices and thought leaders. After a month of comfort and confidence, I proactively connected with a few identified thought-leaders, as it related to book publishing, to request a few minutes of their time for professional guidance and expertise. Not all responded back to me, but many did accept an invitation for a 15-minute call based on my personalized messages that highlighted some of their online interactions. These calls, although I never met the thought-leaders in person, were tremendous. Each person brought me an interesting viewpoint or action for my specific project and many shared best practices and areas to streamline the process. It was a terrific experience for me and accelerated my time to market.

I cannot say enough about all I have gained from these online professional groups and resources over the years. They have contributed to my knowledge, network, results and self-efficacy. Some groups I have followed for almost a decade where others have been important at different career milestones. I would highly encourage you to take the time to find groups and resources that align with where you are and where you want to go next.

If you have trouble finding a group for your niche, check out **Chapter 8: Finding Networking Groups that Work for You**, or consider starting a group yourself. "Why Starting a LinkedIn Group," by Stephanie Sammons shares some of the benefits of starting a group on LinkedIn. Although the article is from 2012, her listed benefits are still valid and many I have experienced firsthand.

After 10 years on the road working for technology-based firms, most headquartered in California, I packed my bags and moved from Atlanta, Georgia, to Cleveland, Ohio. Shortly after I arrived in 2003, I was looking for other women in tech throughout Northeast Ohio and struggled to find a local or online organization to meet my needs. As I mentioned, after years of searching, I gave into my needs and started Tech Savvy Women in 2008 as a LinkedIn Group. I did not feel like I had the time, but I thought the energy it would generate would make it worth it. I did not overthink it, I just asked a few women I knew in technology roles and companies to get together for wine a few times a year.

Not only has it met a business need for me, but this interactive group is all (+)s and (Y)s on my "Power of No" chart. It gave me great energy and created something interesting to talk about in a world of data centers, servers, storage units, bandwidth, speeds, feeds and applications. It has also created great relevance for many women involved within the technology industry and beyond. There are many ways to increase your relevance to enhance your brand. Your strategies should be determined by where you are and where you want to go. It starts with finding your potential niche followed by making the time to align your commitments to expand in your areas of interest.

Think of yourself as a problem-solver and focus on an area you can best build your skills and expertise to create differentiation in the marketplace. These exercises are often not effective if you try to do them alone. Leverage online resources, platforms and tools that are available to make the most of your time. Time is your biggest asset; use it to get to where you want to go.

CHAPTER EIGHT

Finding Networking Groups
that Work for You

Think for a moment. How often do you seek out opportunities to network with new professionals in your organization, field or across your industry? If you are like many professionals I know, schedules are tight, and it is often difficult to squeeze more out of overcommitted schedules. If you have seen some of my keynotes, I often find ways to incorporate the "Power of No," which is the framework we discussed in the last chapter. It has transformed professionals' time and outcomes. I have found that many professional women and men are leveraging my "Power of No" framework to consciously align their "Yeses" to advance their personal and professional initiatives.

There is no doubt networking is an important part of our professional and personal journeys and often a key factor in creating new opportunities. In fact, many studies show that women excel when they are part of a group that allows them to express their concerns, build their confidence and find safety in their professional choices. In the *Harvard Business Review* article "Women Rising: The Unseen Barriers," authors Herminia Ibarra, Robin J. Ely and Deborah M. Kolb highlight the importance of "creating safe identity workspaces."

The article goes on to share:

> *In the upper tiers of organizations, women become increasingly scarce, which heightens the visibility and scrutiny of those near the top, who may become risk-*

> *averse and overly focused on details and lose their sense of purpose. (In general, people are less apt to try out unfamiliar behaviors or roles if they feel threatened.) Thus, a safe space for learning, experimentation, and community is critical in leadership development programs for women.*
>
> *Identifying common experiences increases women's willingness to talk openly, take risks and be vulnerable without fearing that others will misunderstand or judge them. These connections are especially important when women are discussing sensitive topics such as gender bias or reflecting on their personal leadership challenges, which can easily threaten identity and prompt them to resist any critical feedback they may receive.*

When I started Tech Savvy Women, I too needed a "safe place." At that point I had been in the tech industry for 13 years, moving through the ranks, which I now recognize as a common time when women tend to opt out of tech and other STEM jobs. Catherine Ashcraft, Ph.D. and Sarah Blithe of The National Center for Women & Technology, highlight these opt-out stats, along with strategies to retain women in their fields in the article "Women in IT: The Facts."

According to a study by the Center for Work-Life Policy:

> *Seventy-four percent of women in technology report 'loving their work,' yet many of these women leave their careers at a staggering rate: 56 percent of technical women leave at the 'midlevel' point just when the loss of their talent is most costly to companies.*

This is more than double the quit rate for men. It is also higher than the quit rate for women in science and engineering.

I guess I did not fully realize this at the time but I, too, was seeking relatable conversations with professional women who could understand my demanding schedules and aspirations. I was also looking to expand my network and create meaningful professional connections outside of my daily responsibilities in a software company, which was very rewarding, but at times lonely. I worked with many smart and effective people. I appreciated being part of the team, but at times, you could not deny that being one of the only women on the team had its challenges.

I later learned through some trusted relationships that even though I had great results, many senior executives assumed that I was at my max with two young children. Now, after hours of conversations and research, I can see how these related assumptions could have impacted my promotion schedule.

I find it important to note that I have worked with many amazing professionals, most of them men. Many previous co-workers are now friends and some have been my professional sponsors along the way. For the most part, I have had very positive experiences working on teams where I was the only woman.

Building Tech Savvy Women from just a few women to thousands of women all over the world has exceeded any expectations I had when I created it. Through the need to come together with other professional women, I have created wonderful relationships, connected many women to new people and even new job opportunities, all while enjoying great conversations in delightful locations often with delicious wine and food.

Thanks to all the businesses, golf courses, wine bars, nonprofits, restaurants and corporations that hosted and sponsored Tech Savvy Women over the years. These gatherings opened new doors and presented new opportunities. These women gave me strength, encouraged me to explore new paths and were likely the catalysts for my first book, *The Working Woman's GPS*.

In addition to Tech Savvy Women, there are so many wonderful national and international organizations for professional women that are specifically designed to bring purposeful women together for the opportunity to network, connect, advance and learn.

Below is a list of women's organizations, technology associations for women, and organizations and initiatives for girls interested in STEM. This is not even close to a complete list. It is just a glimpse of some of the groups that have crossed my path over the last two decades.

Note: For easy reference, this list along with each organizations' website is located in Appendix B.

I encourage you to ask people you admire about their career path, the groups they value and participate in along the way. Read about local events, join social media groups and find related blogs that share gathering information and details. Become aware of the regional, industry or interest-based initiatives and organizations available to you.

Women's Organizations
American Business Women's Association
Athena International
Working Women Connection
National Association of Women Business Owners
National Association of Female Executives
American Business Women's Association
National Association of Professional Women
The Glasshammer
YWCA
WirL

Women in Technology
Anita Borg Institute
CodeChix
Global Tech Women
Million Women Mentors
NCWIT
NPower
Pink Petro
STEM Connectors
WITI
Women in AV

Technology, Math and Science for Young Women
CampTech
DigiGirlz (Microsoft)
Expanding Your Horizon (AT&T)
Gems Club: Girls Excelling in Math and Science
Girl Geeks
Girl Scouts
Girls Inc.
Girls Who Code
Girls-ology
ID Tech
National Girls Collaboration
Project Lead the Way
Sally Ride Science
STEM.org

STEMgeo
Tech Bridge
Tech Girls
TechPREP
We Can Code IT
Youth Campaign

Before leaving this chapter, spend a few minutes thinking about how you network and what you make time for in your schedule that creates opportunities to meet new professionals and align with where you desire to make an impact next. Here are a few questions to get started:

- What networks or groups am I a part of today?
- How often do I contribute within each group?
- How do I participate beyond membership?
- What benefits do I receive from these networks?
- What new professional connections have I established based on these activities?
- Are there opportunities to create additional synergies and alignment with people in these networks to prepare me for my professional future?

	Network 1	Network 2	Network 3	Network 4
Network/Group				
Your Contribution				
Additional Activities				
Direct Benefits				
Professional Connections				
Additional Synergies				

I have left a few extra lines for you to add a few more details that showcase the benefits, opportunities and even gaps you might be experiencing in your current groups. This chart helps me identify where I need to spend more time and where I need to better align my time.

Networking should have mutual benefits. It's about what you need, but also what you contribute to the others in your network. Conversely, it can't be all about you. The old saying that you get what you give certainly applies to being part of a network. It might not be every meeting or event but across the board, you should see value in what you contribute and what you get in return. By creating a chart, whether you use this one or another format, it should allow you to arrange comparative data to identify gaps and future areas of focus. As we move forward, start to think about what new types of networks you need to join to help pave your future professional path.

CHAPTER NINE

Investing in Your Network

For some, facilitating activities to connect to new people may feel like a chore or even worse, a nightmare. If expanding relationships or connecting to new people is outside your comfort zone, don't fret. There are ways to mask these activities into problem-solving quests that can likely generate the similar results to support your desired level of impact and professional growth.

Let's think about all the people you pass in your day, the events and meetings you attend and people you talk to on the phone. Through these activities, how many people do you think you interact with in a week? Just think, the people you may need to know to help facilitate your path may already be among your existing connections.

An easy approach to enhancing your sphere of mentors and sponsors is expanding your conversations with the people you already connecting with each day. Spend a few minutes more with the people you are already connect with by taking the time to ask them about their professional goals. One of my favorite questions is: "What steps did you take to get into your existing role and who sponsored you along the way?"

Think for a moment:

- Do I know what people do throughout their day in addition to the project they work on with me?
- Do I know about some of their professional passions?
- Do I know where they hope to have more impact?

You may or may not see yourself as naturally inquisitive, but seeking just a little more information about the people you work with each day inside or outside of the office could enhance your professional connections and potentially your trajectory.

As I think about some of my encounters where I have spent a few more minutes asking a few more questions about career paths, desired next steps and goals outside of work, I realize they have steered me to new connections, conversations and even initiatives.

Through these additional questions, you can seek to learn what others are looking to achieve or the relationships or awareness they are working to establish. It might even be possible for you to assist in their journey.

These intentional and authentic requests could be viewed as a problem-solving exercise and spin the potential intimidation factor into a contribution to other's activities. If you adjust your lens and view networking and creating new connections as a problem-solving exercise, you may see networking as an easier and more inviting activity within your schedule to enhance existing connections or make new connections.

As you take time to develop professional relationships, you may start to recognize the patterns, opportunities and gaps in your existing network. Spend time engaging and understanding the different people, viewpoints, backgrounds and goals that already exist with the people you connect with the most.

You may have noticed that I like to sort and organize data to identify patterns, themes, gaps and opportunities. My mind cannot help but to create a system related to my connections too. Even though I recognize that people are different than commitments and some of the other categories I have created charts for in this book.

- **Patterns.** Arrange the types of people you already have in your network by a series of groupings such as current role, professional interests, level of influence, interest in helping you and your ability to help them. It may help you determine where you need additional input, guidance or help.
- **Opportunities.** Identify areas you can connect, share, direct or contribute to the people in you network. These efforts to assist others often give me a boost of positive energy that help carry me through my day and once in a while create future benefits.
- **Gaps.** Determine areas where you need additional assistance. As you spend time with your existing network, with your aspirations in mind, you can likely recognize where you could use some additional help, guidance and connections. Identifying your gaps is possible once you are clear about your

future goals, and you spend more quality time with the people already in your network.

Now you might be thinking that your field of work is small or that you work remotely and there are only a few events a month in your town. You might think that much of your network is made up of the people you work with each day. But think for a moment: There are more people around you in addition to the people you work directly with each day.

I often need help around my house—like adding an outlet, preparing for a holiday event or taking off the window screens—so I can focus my time toward my business projects. So, if you are worried that your business network is tapped, you can potentially add value and minimize your gaps from your network outside of work deliverables.

Araujo's article, which I mentioned earlier, offers some advice on expanding your network:

> The first challenge that you will likely have when it comes to becoming a great connector is that your world is too small... However, to create the Medici Effect, you need to bring together people of different disciplines, cultures, and perspectives. It means that you need to get out of your comfort zone and find people whose backgrounds are different than your own! Perhaps this involves going to a financial industry networking event. Or perhaps you can attend a gallery reception or a fundraiser. Whatever it is, just make sure that you are purposefully putting yourself in a situation where you will meet people who look at the world differently than you do.

In another great resource, posted on Psych Central called "6 Strategies to Make Valuable Work Connections," author Christy Matta shares how to make great connections at work. Within her six strategies are practices I have adopted:

> Attend an industry convention or networking meeting with a plan. Review the presenters ahead of time and map out who you'd like to meet. Prepare a few sentences about their accomplishments or interests and why you want to meet them.

Before I attend or speak at an event, I review the event site a few times, Google the other speakers, read related blog posts and identify key people I am interested in meeting when I am there.

> *Ask questions. It can be intimidating to approach others, but most people like to talk about themselves. Asking questions can prompt a genuine discussion.*

While smiling, I often ask open-ended questions such as: "How did you get into this industry? What attracted you to this event?"

It often only takes a few minutes to establish a rapport with another person. If you happen to stumble upon an unengaging or negative person, which does happen from time to time, politely excuse yourself with "it was so nice to meet you" and move on to explore other conversations.

As for the more engaging professionals that are open to new connections, be sure to collect business cards. Use these after the event to connect via email or LinkedIn. As I mentioned, follow-up is important. Make sure you schedule time the next day—or within the week—to solidify those new connections.

In some cases, people share projects or initiatives with me, and if I have people in my network that have similar initiatives or could potentially help, I offer to connect them after the event.

I primarily make connections between two people via email or within a LinkedIn message.

I prefer LinkedIn since it provides a great overview of experiences and accomplishments so each person can quickly assess the connection.

Acting as a connector is often easy to do if you create conversations that seek information about their initiatives. Knowing more about the people in your network affords you opportunities to connect people who can benefit each other.

If you are still unsure how to add value in this way, observe the people around you. Who do you already know that is great at fostering their network and acting as a connector? Consider taking them out to lunch and ask them about their approach, past successes and hurdles. I say hurdles because not all connections have resulted in a great story. Some connections have fallen flat, but I am not discouraged by these abysses because there have been many connections that have found opportunities to share and advance initiatives.

If you are still not feeling it, consider personal engagements throughout the business day as career investments. Your networks, sponsors and related references can ultimately determine where you go in your career.

I was recently talking to a real estate woman about her business, and she mentioned that she wasn't comfortable attending events because she did not like promoting herself or listening to others gush about their work.

She said, "When I go to a networking event, I do not like initiating a conversation, and I am horrible at leading with my business card to let people know who I am, who I help and how I can help them. I often leave these same events empty handed—not knowing who even attended or what people to follow-up with or who could be a great new person to add to my network."

> Hello Jennifer and Sharon,
>
> One of my favorite things is connecting fantastic women like the 2 of you!
>
> I think there may be synergy between your expertise and existing initiatives.
>
> Sharon, Jennifer is working on some awesome next-generation digital/tech solutions for our community with the support of a few foundations and industry leaders.
>
> Jennifer, Sharon has made her mark bringing great technology ideas to market. She has great perspective and experience helping drive market value and repeatable revenue streams.
>
> I am connecting you via LinkedIn so you can quickly see each other's background and area of focus.
>
> Happy Friday,
> JJ

Many women struggle with these situations. But networking is critical, which is why I found the time to write about it.

Make a point of creating valuable conversations, getting to know the people you cross paths with and finding ways to help. It's a great strategy to reignite your network building activities. Here are a few action-based questions:

- How can I make networking less of a chore?
- What excites me about meeting new people?
- How can I add value to the people I am connected to now?
- What events can I attend to be more relevant and connected?
- What is the best way for me to stay connected and engaged?
- What gaps, obstacles or opportunities could my connections help me overcome?

When you go with the attitude of helping others, most people find interest in you and what you do too.

Don't be surprised if people contact you through LinkedIn, forward your profile or research you online before meeting again. Knowing this, it is important you make time to keep your online profiles up-to-date with an acute focus on your LinkedIn profile—whether you are looking for a job or not.

Online profiles are an easy place to meet and connect with business people around the globe. It has become such a common business practice for people to review your profile before or after meeting you to see what professional milestones you have achieved to date, what you are working on now, who you are connected to and who you are following.

Remember Snyder's article in *Fortune* states: "Women's resumes are longer, but shorter on details than men's." This can apply to LinkedIn profiles, too.

A few things to think about as we wrap up this chapter:

- Am I providing enough detail in my profile to showcase my abilities and outcomes?
- Have I taken the time to describe my current and previous roles with measurable outcomes?
- Do I have indicators based on where I want to go next? Such as people I follow, groups I belong to or new people I am connected to?
- Have I asked for references with LinkedIn?
- Do I have a profile that showcases my professional brand?

CHAPTER TEN

Getting the Most from Organized Events

Some women I know attend events each week, while others may only attend a few events a year. Quantity is not the measuring stick. There does not seem to be a magic number of events, connections or groups. But getting out of your office and away from your to-do list does seem to have merit.

Carol Bartz, in her 2014 *Fortune* article, "Why Women Should Do Less and Network More," states:

> *Women spend more time doing and less time networking. And this is no small matter. In today's market, networking has become the lifeblood of a fruitful professional life... But leadership today is increasingly defined not just by how many hours you spend at your computer, but your ability to connect to others, how you incorporate outside perspectives, and how you navigate groups. Networking takes time, but it matters.*

Depending on where you desire to accelerate your impact, networking and related events may be an essential component and even act as a multiplier as you map out your desired goals. But not all events are the same, so going and signing up for a ton of events may have little to no effect as you work to advance your goals.

The I's of Networking is something I highlight with many executive men and women when they contact me to discuss their professional horizon. I do not proclaim to be an executive coach, but I often get requests for executive exploration calls. During these discussions, we often outline potential milestones based on their professional path to date and where they aspire to create additional impact and influence. It could be their main job, but it is often adjunct activities at work, in the community or around new initiatives.

There are three I's that I suggest when looking to add another commitment in the form of an event to your schedule:

Investigate. Do your research before you agree to attend.
- Investigate the different events in your area by looking at their website, boards, previous events and people who have attended.
- Check out their social media participation, if they have it, and even do a few internet searches for posts and related comments.

Interview. Locate a few people already participating.
- Interview people who already attend some of the events that you are interested in adding to your schedule.
- Understand the perceived value people receive from being part of this network and attending these events.

Identify. List a few potential opportunities or benefits you may experience.
- Identify the value. List a few bullets on why these new networks and events might matter to where you are or where you hope to accelerate your activities and output.
- Many groups meet a few times a year, some meet online and in-person, others have active virtual conversations within online groups and pages. Decide how you plan to engage in this type of group based on your existing commitments.

I have leveraged these I's as champions of impactful schedules and meaningful engagements. It has benefited me, and others, to take the time to assess and understand what it is, who attends and why I should attend.

Using these I's enables you to collect some important details about the group, related events, people who attend and a glimpse of the expectations and potential benefits before you jump in. These insights ahead of time will likely make more effective use of your time and set the right expectations for the initial event.

ART OF NETWORKING

As you have likely heard hundreds of times, there is an art to networking. This section is not written to recreate those best practices. Rather, it is to encourage you to think more about how you spend your time, especially as it relates to building your network and nurturing your professional relationships.

Judy Robinett, author of *How To Be A Power Connector: The 5 + 50 + 150 Rule*, says, "Building a network is about getting in the right room." Taking the time upfront to research and plan, will likely save you time while facilitating more meaningful conversations and potential connections.

If you link Robinett's advice with Madeleine Albright, who says, "I think women are really good at making friends and not good at networking. Men are good at networking and not necessarily making friends. That's a gross generalization, but I think it holds in many ways," it gives you something to think about, especially as it relates to the way you approach events, connections and conversations.

This seems to be a good time to spend a minute and think about how you network and who you network with in addition to your team or teams. I know it is not always easy to stretch in new directions or approach a new person, but let's take a look at what has worked for you to date. I know each day and event is different, but for these few questions, think about the times when you were on, which is when you felt great and your actions align with your positive energy:

- When do I do a good job networking and connecting with new people?
- What common behaviors or themes occur during these effective situations?
- How can I expand into new spheres of influence while still maintaining some comfort in my actions?

GO WITH A PURPOSE

Working a room may have a different meaning today than it did a few years ago, especially with the increased availability of information online. When attending a function, there are some techniques I have leveraged to get the most out of an event.

If you can, get a list of the people attending before you arrive at the event or spend time reviewing the "plan to attend" list. Identifying the people who plan to be in the room is helpful if you desire to meet a few key people. I often select three to five people I hope to meet at a specific event, which gives me a purpose when I attend. Setting this type of goal also encourages me to move away from my comfort zone of mingling with people I already know. If there is no online or available list, look at the speakers or companies sponsoring the event and see if you can build a plan to make some worthy connections.

If you have room in your budget, you can always offer to sponsor the entire event or even a portion such as the appetizers, room costs or desserts. With this investment, you sometimes get a few minutes to talk about your work and/or company or even include a short description in the agenda. This way, people know who you are before you attend, giving you additional opportunities to make connections. If you have the opportunity to make an investment in a desired event, you can often ask the event planner to personally introduce you to specific people, a type of attendee or other sponsors.

If you have some time, you can write or share details about the event with your network using related hashtags and Twitter accounts that can potentially cultivate new conversations with others planning to attend the event. I have been known to write a focused blog for a specific event. With this, I often talk to the event host before posting to see if there are any items they want highlighted or referenced. This conversation often gives me insight to the agenda, attendees and desired outcome.

If you work for a company that has logo-based material such as pens, pads or other items you can offer to donate them for attendees' gift bags or event raffles. These are just some of the ways to get your information in front of many attendees, potentially opening pathways to connect with new people.

If you are unsure the best way to engage, you could go to the event first to get a feel for the event and attendees, then make a plan for the second event. Many approaches can be effective based on how much time you have in your schedule, your related interest, available resources and how quickly you want to meet your goals. When you attend events, here are a few things to keep in mind as you approach new people:

Be an Effective Listener: In Stephen Covey's *The 7 Habits of Highly Effective People*, "Habit 5: Seek First to Understand, Then to

Be Understood" is a popular phrase and very applicable to the first stage of networking:

> *Because most people listen with the intent to reply, not to understand. You listen to yourself as you prepare in your mind what you are going to say, the questions you are going to ask, etc. You filter everything you hear through your life experiences, your frame of reference. You check what you hear against your autobiography and see how it measures up. And consequently, you decide prematurely what the other person means before he/she finishes communicating.*

Actively listening can easily help you recall information such as names, companies, roles, goals and desires allowing you to actively help if you have the knowledge, experience or connections in your network.

Find Themes to Make Worthy Connection: Inevitably, once you understand a person's role and/or goals, you may think of someone that they should meet. You might say something like "Have you met so and so? I think you two need to know each other."

Coordinate Connections: Take the time to make connections after the event with people you meet. If there is a good reason to connect two people in your network, take the time to do so. There can be great long-term benefits from these types of connections and related synergies. These direct connections will not only advance their network and maybe their business, but could be beneficial to you too.

Just last month, I was speaking at a STEM conference for educators and met another speaker—let's call him John. John was working on many initiatives including an electrical plane. As he was talking, another person in my network, let's call him Steve, had similar interests that came to mind. Even though John lives in California and Steve lives in Florida, I thought it would be helpful to connect them. I could have sent an email since I had both their email addresses, but opted for LinkedIn so they could both see each other's backgrounds, work experience and related networks.

After I had made this initial connection, John and Steve connected with each other online and via a call. Funny enough, John was scheduled to speak near Steve's town, and they were able to meet in person. These two people easily found a few ways to advance each other's projects. In fact, a notable event occurred—Steve connected John to a new product distributor to advance the development of his electrical plane.

In separate conversations, John and Steve shared their appreciation for this connection. Now not all connections work out this way, but what do you think would happen if I called either one of them for advice, help or a connection to someone in their networks?

There are multiple ways to create mutual benefits within your existing network and with new people. Hopefully, you have some newfound benefits, strategies and tools as you harvest existing networks and participate in new events.

I am a believer that with a plan, networking in new places is not wasted time. In fact, Bartz shares in her article a great finding: "Don't believe that time spent networking hurts productivity. Data by International Data Corporation and the McKinsey Global Institute has shown that 28 percent of our working week is spent reading, deleting, filing and sending emails, and 19 percent is spent searching and gathering information." View these activities as an important part of your week, which aligns with searching and gathering data.

Bartz, the former CEO of Yahoo and Autodesk, goes on to share:

> *Networking not only expands business opportunities within company walls and externally. It creates that space where professional boundaries are softened by personality, often paving the way for women to be more effective in driving initiatives forward in the workplace. It allows women to find role models and business leads not available inside their office. Most important, social connection and professional engagement is what makes our jobs interesting and enduring.*

Attending organized events in new ways can take some practice. Be diligent about what events you attend and don't forget to do your I's:

- **Investigate:** Do your research before you agree to attend.
- **Interview:** Locate a few people already participating.
- **Identify:** List a few potential opportunities or benefits you may experience.

After you select an event, have a purpose, research the people attending and lead with a true desire to get to know the people you meet—be ready to share who you are and what you desire. People seem to remember those that truly listen and help them along their professional path.

In return for your mindshare and time, many, not all, will be gracious enough to ask you about you and your business goals. "Gosh, thanks for your help. So what is it that YOU do?" It often does not take long for people to recognize that you are willing and interested in their work and desired next steps. Be ready to share who you are and what you desire.

I help _____ advance ____(a verb)____ for/to _____.
I am looking to get involved in _____
and need help with _____.

After you leave, follow-up with the people you met. If you can make some synergistic connections, go for it. It may take some time, but what I have learned is that there are often many hidden treasures in and outside your existing network. Investing the time to effectively network can often lead you to some gems.

CHAPTER ELEVEN

Engaging Catalysts: Mentors, Sponsors and Advisory Boards

Many of us desire a broader scope of influence and impact but often have not been able to solely manifest these desires and related opportunities. Just as athletes need coaches and companies need PR experts, individuals need career catalysts at different points along the way.

Some professionals are very specific on where they desire to go next and where they aspire to be in three to five years. Other professionals are not as clear on what success looks like for them and what the next step in their journey will be or perhaps even what it should be. Taking the time to create clarity is an important step for any professional if they aspire for new experiences and areas of impact.

It is possible you have determined that achieving the clarity you desire is difficult to do alone. Or, you have clarity, and you have not been able to catapult in the direction you desire. What I have learned is that both of these activities—gaining clarity on your desired next step and manifesting it—require insight, guidance and help from others. I categorize this help in the form of career catalysts.

In many ways it is like assembling a project team to determine if this is something you can achieve on your merit and past successes or if you need to engage others to help catapult you forward faster than you can move alone.

Coaches, mentors, sponsors and advisory boards are types of career catalysts. Of course, each type of career catalyst can have different levels of impact on you and your career. As your professional scope and desires evolve, the people who can help you along the way may change as well.

To be sure we are synced on the differences, let me define the types of catalysts you might encounter or develop through your professional journey.

A COACH

A coach is often a hired professional who helps you define, align and move toward your professional goals. I suggest investing in a coach when you need honest advice, clarity and a plan. The role of a coach is to organize your desires, experiences and next steps so that you can effectively articulate your accomplishments, current impact and future aspirations to your non-hired career catalysts—often called mentors and sponsors.

A coach works with you to help you gain clarity on your desired outcomes, which could be a new project, a board seat or a promotion among other titles and roles. Coaches can also help you align action-based steps to create new levels of impact and influence.

A MENTOR

A mentor is typically not hired, but is often a person who gives you advice on how to move from here to there or maneuver a situation. They often share their opinions and sometimes their contacts. The conversation usually consists of what you could do or how you might approach or respond to the current situation. Often these mentoring sessions are confined by the time you are together and once the conversation is over, you both move on with your day.

A word of advice: You should only disclose confidential information to a select group of people. Not everyone has your best interest in mind, so be cautious about what you share and how often you share it to be sure people are not undermining your efforts, taking your ideas or wasting your time.

A SPONSOR

A sponsor is a person who talks to you about your goals and guides you in a productive direction, which is similar to a mentor. But a sponsor takes it a step beyond mentorship, using his or her ability to tap into their social capital to position or endorse you to others. The key words here are social capital. In most situations, it's advantageous to have a person who understands your professional goals, attitude and outcomes to champion you to people who are or are not familiar with you and your work. This can provide you another level or validation and endorsement.

Sponsors are often known to help facilitate desired next steps directly or indirectly by highlighting your skills, accomplishments and contributions to the "right" people in their networks to help you catapult in your desired direction.

Let's think about your sponsors for a minute:
- How many sponsors do I have right now?
- Are they familiar with my accomplishments?
- Do my sponsors know the work I have been doing to become more relevant, connected and aligned?
- Are they aware of where I want to go next?
- Have any of my sponsors leveraged their social capital to help accelerate my goals?

Your sponsors, which we will discuss in more detail in the next chapter, can be a critical piece to your future alignment. If you are panicking right about now, don't be alarmed. I meet many women who are not sure who in their network are mentors and who are sponsors. The next few chapters will help you organize and align with what you need moving forward.

AN ADVISORY BOARD

An advisory board is an assembly of people within your inner circle upon whom you call for advice, guidance and elevation. These are often a gathering of coaches, mentors and sponsors. My mentors and sponsors have been significant in all aspects of my life. Like everything, there is a place and time, and most of my mentors and sponsors have come and gone. Many have left me with lifelong imprints of their generosity, support and impact. I am grateful and honored to be supported by so many amazing people.

When I started Tech Savvy Women, I invited a few senior women in my network who trusted me. I leveraged my advisory board to provide advice on how to kick it off and to keep it going beyond one meeting. I contacted women in tech, people in human resources and leaders of other women's groups in other cities. I needed guidance and support, which is why people on my advisory board were fabulous mentors, sponsors and coaches to start Tech Savvy Women.

As you can imagine, these relationships take a level of commitment from both sides. Women (and men) must actively develop productive and reciprocal relationships and honor the gift of their time and energy.

As with any relationship or partnership, there needs to be a mutual benefit for everyone involved. Many of us are looking to grow and broaden our skills, talents and impact. For some, that can be achieved through helping others. A professional relationship could be as simple as a leader wanting to invest in someone of the same gender, community or department to ensure success. Through their effort, there are many benefits to the individual, leader and company. Working to identify the value for all parties is significant in developing an effective working relationship.

Last year, a midcareer woman responsible for a large bank's online banking portal contacted me. She asked me, "Do I need male mentors?" My response for most broad questions was, "Well, it depends." She paused, and I added, "Tell me more about what are you working to accomplish?"

The conversation often breaks open after this type of question, and the person on the other end of the phone usually streams a series of thoughts. Because there is so much to this topic, I have included an in-depth exercise in **Chapter 3: Bundling Your Value** with a specific focus on these three areas:

Accomplishments + Current Impact + Future Aspirations

After a 25-minute conversation, we circled back with an answer based on her original question: "Working in most high-impact environments can be lonely, especially if you are one of the only women. Taking time to create effective mentors and sponsors often helps professional women avoid isolation and common career potholes. I would almost always say yes, it is important for your sanity and growth to have at least one mentor and one sponsor. Gender may or may not matter, but I believe it is more important to align with people who have some level of social capital based on your professional goals. In your case, and in your industry, male mentors and sponsors will likely be very helpful. If your time and interest allow it, work to create an advisory board."

Knowing advisory boards take some planning and time, it is ideal to create a thought-diverse group of people around you. Striving for different backgrounds, gender, age and experience inside and outside of your department, company and industry is ideal.

In Gwen Moran's Fast Company article, "Should Women Seek Male Mentors?," Pamela McCauley, a professor in the Department of Industrial Engineering and Management Systems at the University of Central Florida, says "she reminds women that men often face similar challenges balancing work and family, and may bring fresh perspectives about managing those challenges."

The topics of gender and career catalyst often appear as a popular question from professional women: "Do you have male mentors and sponsors?" My usual answer: "Yes, with a 20-year career in high tech, most of my mentors and sponsor were and still are men of all ages and different industries." I am fortunate that as I have professionally evolved, so has my advisory board. Just recently, I have had more women within my advisory board.

In the same *Fast Company* article, McCauley shares:

> *Instead of focusing on gender, women should be asking several key questions to find the right mentor:*
> * *Is this person successful enough to help me advance in my career?*
> * *Does this person understand the mentoring process?*
> * *How does this person interact with women?*
> * *Is this person a good teacher?*
> * *Is this person willing to help and be enthusiastic about devoting the time it will take to be a mentor?*

Her bottom line: "Your mentor has to want to invest some time in you to be effective."

I am so honored and grateful to the many people—men and women, although most have been men—who have taken an interest in my career path over the last 25 years. I have had some fabulous mentors and sponsors at different times that have showed up in unique ways. Looking back, there was often more than one person who helped me create, clarify, define and prepare for what was next.

Sponsors, mentors and advisory boards are people interested in helping you identify and achieve your professional dreams and aspirations. Your mindset going into these relationships can make a huge difference. You need to think about how you can reciprocate to them or others while having clarity on your own goals to maximize your time together.

It is often important to align with your talents and marketable skills, but you should be just as enthusiastic about addressing your weaknesses that may be holding you back from catapulting in the direction you desire. If you're unclear about those shortcomings, invest in yourself, hire a coach or partner-up with someone within your advisory board to identify your gaps with a goal to overcome the areas that could help you leap in your desired direction.

It may be easy to say: "Well I cannot find a mentor or sponsor" or "I do not need an advisory board." But it's like saying, "I don't need a team, I can play this game solo," when the game is really a team sport. Finding your career catalysts is like Popeye finding his spinach.

WHO TO HAVE ON YOUR ADVISORY BOARD

Coach, Mentor or Sponsor	Qualities	Potential Actions to Help You	Reciprocal Actions to Help Them	Now, Next or Both

Coach/Mentor/Sponsor: List a few of your mentors, sponsors or coaches.
Qualities: Next to each name, list a few of this person's qualities as it relates to your meetings, discussions and actions.
Potential Actions to Help You: For each person, list potential actions they could do to help you.
Reciprocal Actions to Help Them: List actions you are able to do for this person.
Now, Next or Both: Is this person well-suited for where you are now? Where you plan to go next? Or both?

Now that you have a better idea of the people who make up your advisory board today, it is easier to recognize your champions and how they might be able to help you move in your desired direction. Within that same thread, it is also possible that you now see some potential gaps. Taking time to identify ways you can round out your advisory board with a few more people is a great next step.

CHAPTER TWELVE

Identifying Your Sponsors

I was at a fabulous dinner just a few weeks before finishing this book with a dear friend who is an awesome connector, among many other things. She invited me to dinner to make a connection to an established and experienced woman in the technology field. I was honored and excited for this new connection.

We discussed the topics I was including in this book. At one point, she asked me: "What is one thing that a woman can do to help advance her career?" Without hesitation, I answered: "Align with sponsors." Her smile grew, which was a clear indicator that I was on the mark.

Whether we know it or not, we each have sponsors in our life that aid us in various ways and times. The question is: Do we know who these people are and are we effectively investing in these relationships?

Let's review in case you are not reading chapter by chapter.

WHAT IS A SPONSOR?

A sponsor is someone in your network that can create connections for you, lead you to important information or help you avoid potential pitfalls based on their experience, network, viewpoint and knowledge of you.

If you are a professional businesswoman looking to advance your career within your industry, make a more meaningful impact in your existing role or break into a new line of work, access to relevant sponsors could be critical to your next steps.

Many of your future career advancements could require someone else facilitating and promoting you within critical conversations and situations in which you may not be privy too.

A sponsor could be your boss, a business partner, an established business owner in your community, a neighborhood friend or any number of other people in your network. Once you align with potential sponsors, you must create ways to share your career desires and goals while offering to reciprocate in areas that create benefits for your sponsor.

Now this might be intimidating, but this reciprocation could be easy. If you're thinking what can I offer, there are many ways you can reciprocate that are often not much work compared to the value you will receive from this professional relationship. For example, a sponsor of mine asked me to have a few calls with his niece that was in a computer program and looking to talk with a woman in the field. Another sponsor asked me to help on a committee for young adults in need of college tuition and another asked me to deliver great results in my next role that directly benefited his team and goals.

A word of caution, some of these professional-based relationships are short-lived. Many can change as the environments or desired expectations change, which is why networking with new people in new ways is such a critical piece of your professional evolution.

Let's jump into how to identify your sponsors.

STEP ONE: DEFINE YOUR GOALS

Before you jump in, take a step back to understand what you have achieved to date and then outline your future goals. As we discussed in the previous chapter, what professional milestones or notable outcomes have you achieved in your career?

Reflect on your notes from these questions stated earlier in the book to identify your key milestone from previous roles and engagements:

- What are my most important projects in the last five to seven years?
- What significant accomplishments have I achieved during this time?
- What special projects were assigned to me?
- Why was I assigned to these projects?
- What obstacles was I able to overcome during these projects?
- What where the known milestones or related metrics in which I was measured?
- What kind of recognition did I receive?

It is important to document your accomplishments along the way because life moves fast and we often forget some of the significant details that can set us apart in future situations. To expand on the earlier questions, think about the work you do today and the related results:
- What value do I provide in my current role?
- Who can speak of the work I do today?
- How would people describe my contributions?
- Who could I call on to be a reference or sponsor?

Now add some parameters around where and how you want to accelerate your impact:
- What additional level impact and influence am I striving for?
- Who is already delivering these types of results?
- Can I create a bridge from my existing network and work to where I aspire to go next within my professional sphere?
- Do I need to create new connections to help build this professional bridge?
- Can most people see me stretch in this direction?

Organizing your credentials based on where you are and where you want to go is important to identify where you need help and sponsorship. Many women have a hard time articulating "an ask," whether it is sponsorship for a new role, a project request, a recommendation or a connection. With this data, you can work to map out your needs. If your need more help outlining all the pieces, I suggest a professional or executive coach to help you plot out your goals, gaps and next steps. It is likely you will have some help clarifying your *ask*, which is important to catapulting toward your goals.

An ask is as simple as asking someone with professional clout to help in your professional journey. As I mentioned earlier, people with social capital can be a huge asset. I often think of someone with professional clot as someone who also has social capital.

An essential factor for women with an ask is asking people who can help facilitate conversations, connections and opinions. *Women often do a good job at networking with their peers or with people who report to them, but they often don't do as good a job networking above their existing level where people may have additional professional clout and social capital to help accelerate the desired path.*

Mentors have their role and can often provide value, but for most women, they need more than a group of mentors. Many women need sponsors—people who have social capital and are willing to help manifest future goals.

HIRING A PROFESSIONAL COACH

Before marching off to find your sponsors or scheduling time with your existing sponsors, I suggest engaging a professional friend to review your plans and desires. Better yet, invest in a career coach to help you build your ask based on your professional goals. It often pays off to get an unbiased opinion along with guidance before you meet with your sponsors. It is likely that you will want to ask different people on your advisory board different things and even ask for different levels of connections or sponsorship. Organizing your plan and actions will help foster productive meetings.

As you can tell, I am an advocate and customer of many executive coaches. I have found that it has helped me:

- Brainstorm on what is possible.
- Identify my gaps.
- Strengthen my overall goals.
- Outline specific steps.
- Increase my confidence to schedule time with key stakeholders that can help me pave a path to achieve my desired goals.

If you are wondering where or how to find a professional coach, I suggest asking people in your network that you admire, or that have paved a similar path that you are interested in traveling.

Many successful coaches are interested in establishing effective and productive relationships.

Therefore, many often offer a free 15- to 30-minute consultation to share their approach and determine if there is a natural synergy.

Don't be afraid to schedule a few consultations with different coaches. Not everyone hits it off, so it is helpful to meet with a few different coaches to determine which one is a good fit for you and your desired goals. This is advice I wish I had a few coaches ago.

One time, I hired a very well-known and expensive coach with high hopes to create a working framework to get from where I was to where I wanted to go. He was a referral, and when I reached out to chat with him, his assistant said I needed to pay for his time. He did not offer an initial consultative session—that should have been a clear sign.

The first two meeting were good enough in the sense that he shared lots of successes and asked some good questions, but I started to sense that he was more interested in impressing me with his previous client list. Since I already hired him, I was sold on that, but he could never let that go.

As we continued into the third one-hour session, I found he spent more time talking about himself and his successes than about my goals. I was frustrated. He was expensive and I was getting very little results from our time together. I wanted to end our coaching relationship, but he had a tough contract to break.

Luckily, or not so luckily, he was coaching another woman I knew. I contacted her to see how her coaching sessions were going. I thought maybe I was doing something wrong. Much to my surprise, the coach shared some very personal and private information about me with her that he gathered in our session. There was no other way she could have obtained this information, so I had "good reason" to end our contract.

During our fourth session, I met with him to share these unfortunate findings. He denied it, but I knew he leaked it because my friend went as far to tell me that he told her. I demanded to end our contract with a full reimbursement of the unused sessions. He continued to deny it, but a few days later I received a voicemail from his assistant and shortly after a reimbursement check.

Since then I have not paid a coach or most anyone else in full. I happily pay in stages or based on milestones. I am also now more aware of the cancellation terms and not embarrassed or afraid to add terms of my own if I run into similar unproductive scenarios. As an entrepreneur, I am very leery of lengthy contracts and full upfront payment. I share this only to help you avoid similar pitfalls.

I am happy to say that all the other coaches I have hired along the way have been awesome. They pride themselves on results and often work on fee-based milestones or time committed.

Having clarity on the key milestones of where you have been, what you do now and where you are planning to go next is critical for anyone to help you. Since many, high-impact sponsors are very busy and often overcommitted, the easier you can make it for them to help you, the more likely you are to receive the attention and action you desire.

STEP TWO: IDENTIFY POTENTIAL SPONSORS

It is important to identify people in your life that could help pave the way to get there. If you are looking to grow within the company, look around and identify the people others look to for answers or guidance.

Watch for people who support thought diversity and professional growth of others. Get to know these people. Identify opportunities for them to become familiar with your work and related value to their initiatives and the organization's goals.

I am often researching and reading career-based information about professional women—especially women in tech and related fields. The available research and associated white papers with the related findings have provided me—and many in my network—with so much insight, advice and guidance. One of my favorite publications is "Women in Technology: Leaders for Tomorrow," by Melissa J. Anderson, Nicki Gilmour and Mekayla Castro, which was a cooperation between Accenture and The Glasshammer published by Evolved People Media LLC 2013.

There are so many great insights and data points that I could incorporate from this 20-page publication. I encourage you to take some time to read it as it has brought some clarity and awareness to our world, desires, obstacles and opportunities.

According to the survey:

> *Over three-quarters (77 percent) of the women who responded said they had heard the term 'sponsorship' before, but only a quarter (25.5 percent) of our respondents said they had a sponsor.*

When asked the most desired leadership development courses, "How to connect to a sponsor" ranked No. 3.

I hope these chapters will help you define the steps that will work for you to identify and tap into your sponsors based on where you desire to accelerate your career.

Note, your future sponsor might not have a leadership title or even manage a team, but he or she could be instrumental in paving the way for others to succeed with their social capital.

There are many places to discover sponsors. Once you have investigated your options within your company, look outside your company—expand your circles to meet people who are well-established in the business world, known in the community and active in some nonprofit organizations or industry associations.

STEP THREE: BE PATIENT

The reality is you are not going to be able to get everybody you want to get when it comes to sponsors and/or mentors. Many times, you have to participate in a group for a while before you can get coffee with the people you think can be instrumental in helping you reach your goals.

With these connections and hopefully future sponsors in mind, work now to align with the right networking initiatives, to the right industry initiatives, and to the groups that echo, shadow or showcase where you want to have additional impact in the future. The reason I always say impact and influence is that I have learned many times that not all women want to go up. A lot of women are very happy in their current job but still desire to make a more meaningful impact in their existing role, community or industry as a whole.

Within your action-based plan, take time to outline a targeted approach to find people who have some alignment to where you desire to have more influence and impact next. You can get advice from anybody. But it's helpful to get advice and ideas from people who have already been there or have insight into what's happening in the circle that you want to play in.

Networking in the right circles can help you identify people who can show you the ropes and potentially open doors that you perceive as being closed. I often refer to this as helping you move the chess pieces in your professional trajectory.

Keep in mind, women are more known to network at the same level while men network with people at many levels with an emphasis on upward connections. Just keep this in mind as you enter an event or ask someone for coffee. Ask yourself, *"Am I stretching beyond my comfort zone or am I playing it safe?"*

Check out recent videos on www.TechSavvyWomen.TV, especially the "Career Advancement: Networking Advice for Women in Tech," where I highlight some of the networking challenges and opportunities women experience with suggestions to expand your networking efforts beyond what you are comfortable with today.

Now note, not all people are eager to help you and some people have been successful helping very few. It is likely you will hear your fair shares of "no" or "I don't have time" or even be blown off a few times. Keep your head high and keep at it. I am not suggesting it is easy, but being on a work island, alone, is not easy either.

If you are still scared to stretch into new circles or have put yourself out there with few results, consider trying again with this approach. To get your ego and mind prepared for these networking situations, keep your thoughts focused on your next level of desired impact and influence.

I often trick myself when I feel like all my efforts are amounting to almost nothing. I focus on the goal and my celebration of getting to my next desired step. I envision myself at that moment in time where it is a reality. These visuals often keep my mind focused on the goal and the positive energy I feel when I get that invitation to take on my desired professional goals.

These visualization exercises of envisioning you at the point in time when you have achieved your goal may not jazz you up. If this is the case, take the time to find your personal drivers—reasons you desire to have this additional level of impact or influence. At different times in my life, it has helped to create a vision board. Pictures, sayings or thoughts that keep me focused on where I desire to have the most impact in my life. I have placed them somewhere that it is easy to see, like my bathroom counter, car visor or closet mirror.

Keeping the end in mind, think about what you will feel like and what you will experience once you make your professional goals a reality. These activities that focus on the goal and not the individual activities necessary to get there, helped me not get too caught up on potential or existing potholes along the way.

The more work you put in upfront to define your goals, the easier it is to determine who can help pave the path. Let's revisit a few focus areas to help you recall where you have been and where you desire to go:

- Highlights from previous roles and engagements.
- Daily commitments with a focus on my results.
- Insight to where and how I want to accelerate my impact.

All of these data points should help point you to sponsors that could help you facilitate the right activities, connections and focus areas to increase awareness, relevance and impact. Expanding existing relationships and establishing these new business relationships are key steps for your future journey.

Finding time to cherish your focus and the people you meet along the way is often the fruits of your labor. Like any good role, some relationships are short lived while others last decades. Nurture yourself, your path and all that travels with you.

CHAPTER THIRTEEN

Tapping Into Your Sponsors

Taking time to define your goals with specific details around why and how you can create your desired impact can act as a professional compass. It also can act as a tool to help you articulate where you are now and where you are looking to increase your impact next.

I am not suggesting that this is an easy process. As I mentioned, it unfolded over a series of months where I needed some executive coaching sessions, time to journal, conversations with friends and meetings with professional confidants, to condense years of experience. These activates along with many of the strategies highlighted in previous chapters helped me intertwined previous results, professional desires and life goals into a condensed story I could easily share with mentors and sponsors.

The next few chapters include activities that now act as a framework to identify and effectively access sponsors to pave a path with the help of their knowledge, network, guidance and social capital.

In the last chapter, we covered, Step One: Define Your Goals, Step Two: Identify Potential Sponsors and Step Three: Be Patient. In this chapter, we will cover Step Four.

STEP FOUR: CREATE OPPORTUNITIES TO CONNECT
Make time to establish a more meaningful conversation with potential sponsors. If you already have some level of a relationship with a sponsor, think about your recent conversations. Did they talk more in generalities or did you discuss specific actions and outcomes? Planning your conversation before it happens is something I learned in a sales-based role. It starts with knowing your

desired outcomes before you enter the meeting so when you are leaving the meeting your sponsors have material to champion you in the right direction. From this, creating questions and comments that will help foster the conversation toward a desired end state. The idea is more about cultivating a relevant conversation to ensure you get the most out of your time together.

Start small: Reach out to a person you think could be influential to your goals via email or phone to schedule time.

Keep it simple: Suggest grabbing a cup of coffee or scheduling a 15-minute call.

Refrain from too much too fast: Resist showing up and jumping right into your goals. Instead, work on getting reacquainted on their recent milestones, future goals and interest. As we discussed at the beginning of the book, if this person is a potential sponsor they will ask reciprocal questions about you, your work and your goals.

Not sure who to contact? Start with people who fit some of these characteristics:

- You admire their career path.
- You respect their business decisions.
- You seek to learn more about their career choices.
- You found them as an influencer in your research.
- You have people who have pointed you toward this person.
- You already work with them and appreciate their style.

Not everyone is going to say "yes" to your request so be prepared for some to say "no." Be sure, however, to keep working toward meaningful connections that have the potential to foster into sponsors. Now you might not know who is and is not going to be a sponsor, which is okay. Work to identify people who seem to fit based on your knowledge of them, their work and your goals. It is likely you will have a great conversation at the very least.

Be prepared to ask authentic questions, be curious and be grateful for their time. To prepare for the meeting review their online profiles and recent posts. Have three to five questions based on your desired outcomes that incorporate your research, their knowledge and their career path. Even incorporate some "how did you" question, such as:

- How did you jump from your last position to this position?
- How did you get on   (a board, committee or project) ?

* How did you land __(a specific role)__?
* How did you get the sponsorship you needed along the way?

Like any good meeting, it is always helpful to be prepared with content to guide the conversation. Remember to ask how you can help their initiatives before launching into how they can help you and your specific goals.

It may not seem appropriate to do any asking during this first meeting, especially if you are just starting to develop a rapport. It may even take a few meetings before asking seems appropriate. Even if asking seems awkward, be ready to share your **accomplishments, current impact** and **future aspirations** as part the conversation.

If asked, be sure you can effectively articulate your goals and desired next steps. Being clear and confident is critical—many of these influential sponsors are busy and want something tangible that they can assist with if they can. If you are reading out of order, please be sure to make it back to **Chapter 3: Bundling Your Value.**

If you had an effective meeting, but did not get an opportunity to position an ask, such as:

* What is your advice on X?
* Do you know someone that can X?
* Can you connect me to X?
* Can you sponsor me for this particular position?

Find ways to stay connected—this person may be a future sponsor. Offer to help with one of their initiatives, connect them to a person that can help them and offer to buy coffee again.

Note: It is not necessary to ask "will you be my sponsor." Their actions will speak for themselves.

If your sponsor is someone you already have a mature rapport with, they may be open to scheduling a monthly or quarterly meeting to map out your next steps to help make your goals a reality. These meetings could be just a 15-minute call. The easier you make the request, the more likely people will accept.

For example: "Thanks John for you time today, you really helped me _____. I benefited from our time, could we schedule a 15-minute call next month where I can share my progress and get your perspective on my related activates?"

A woman I worked with years ago, Brandy, called me just before I started working on this book. She was excited to share her professional advancement with me but also wanted to share her disappointment that her sponsor was leaving the company.

Her sponsor was fantastic. Over the years, he had pushed her, championed her and supported her.

It was not too long ago when Brandy left me a voice message to share that she was in the final stages of an interview process for a senior sales positions. I was surprised and excited for her based on the work she was doing when we parted ways—she was an inside sales person. When we connected, I asked her "How did you inject yourself into this process?"

I was very eager to hear how she aligned herself to this position, as it was a very uncommon and often unsupported career path based on the company's culture. The company was all over the technology scene, and this sponsor could easily attract many exceptional and experienced outside sales executives with existing relationships and results.

Much to my surprise, she shared her two-year process that started when she proactively scheduled time with the hiring manager for this position to talk about her career goals.

She did mention that this hiring manager said, "So many come to me with similar requests, but few do the legwork to make this a reality." She took this as a personal challenge as she had her mind set on obtaining this role, which was a huge leap from where she was on the organizational chart when they met. She was, however, more than capable to do the work and excel in this new role.

Brandy continued to share that she proactively scheduled monthly meetings with this hiring manager—he eventually became an instrumental sponsor in her career. I should mention that this was not her existing boss, although she was transparent with him before she actively pursued this new position.

The future boss outlined milestones each sales quarter, and Brandy worked diligently on her day job as to not lose momentum in addition to meeting these additional milestones to position herself as a potential candidate.

Brandy continued to schedule 15 minutes each month where she would come with detailed tasks and actions that she worked through each month in addition to her day job. Months turned into a year, and when a position became available, the hiring manager commended all her work and asked her to interview.

She was the only woman who interviewed. The competition was composed of all men who held similar titles in other companies. After weeks of interviewing, she learned the budget was pulled, and the role was no longer going to be filled that fiscal year.

Disappointed and frustrated, Brandy continued to do her day job, and the hiring manager shared his frustration and condolences. Not giving up, she continued to showcase momentum and impact in her monthly meeting with the hiring manager. He was eager to continue these meetings because he too wanted her to stay excited and engaged in the company as she demonstrated great skills, character and results. They both waited for additional funds to bring her on his team.

More than a month passed, and Brandy found out she was pregnant, but was reluctant to share her news in hopes the job she desired was funded and reposted for potential candidates to apply. She continued to deliver great results in her existing job and after six months she had shared her exciting news in more ways than one. Although excited about her delivery, she was concerned about how she would be perceived at work.

A few weeks before her delivery during her monthly one-on-one meeting with the hiring manager, he shared the news that the job was funded again. He could sense her disappointment. She assumed that she would no longer be considered based on her upcoming maternity leave. But he was required to start the interview process from scratch, which meant new candidates, new expectations and new decision-makers. He went out of his way to provide great support and feedback on her work to date.

Well, I could share the rest in gurgling detail of late nights, finance issues and vice president's 11th-hour disapproval, but none of this matters because the hiring manager was her sponsor. For years, he was her champion.

In the eyes of his peers and leadership, he took a professional gamble when he hired Brandy into an outside sales position while she was on maternity leave. For him, it was not a gamble at all. He invested in her, and she invested in his goals, company, the role and her future.

Her daughter is now almost 3 years old, and she has delivered great results every quarter within her new sales manager role. Her professional relationships have blossomed based on her tenacity, professional vision and results. Yes, it was likely uncomfortable for her to request that first meeting with the hiring manager outside of her direct team. He could have overlooked her, and she could have been embarrassed and unsupported, but she took the gamble and reached out to a person that not only had a role she desired but also the social capital to get her in it.

I have learned so much from Brandy's professional investment. Ask yourself:

- What will you take away from Brandy's story?
- Will you reach out to someone new based on this story?
- How will you think outside the culture that you are currently in?

Among other things, I took away that although these initial requests can be scary and uncomfortable, there are people willing to support your goals, invest in relationships and even take time to help you get there if you show up prepared and ready to do the work.

Tapping into potential sponsors with focused efforts to enhance relationships, identify opportunities and identify benefits can help you pave the way to manifest your professional desires.

BUILDING YOUR TEAM: PLAYER RECAP

Coach. Usually a hired professional to help you get clarity around how you can make additional impact in your existing roles and/or define where you desire to create new levels of impact and influence which could be a new project, board seat or promotion. I hired a coach as I was positioning for my next position. I wanted to be sure I was professionally prepared before engaging my sponsors to help me pave the path.

Mentor. Usually not hired, a mentor is a person in your network that you often trust to share your goals, project or obstacles. A mentor often gives you advice, listens to your ideas and even makes suggestions on ways to move forward. Your conversations are usually inclusive of or bound to the time you are together. In my career, I have leveraged my mentors to validate a career direction or desired plan, understand my potential obstacles, get insight to finish a project or suggestions on other people I should consider engaging in my process or project.

Sponsor. Usually more than a mentor, it is someone that goes beyond the conversation by using his or her social capital to help you pave your path. It is someone who invests in you and your goals at some level by helping you achieve your goals. I have been fortunate to have people in my network that choose to make time to help me increase my level of impact by making a phone call, sending an email or championing me in a meeting. One time, I was working diligently to get into a new group and my existing team was not thrilled for me to leave my existing position. It was a new sponsor that helped me define the right actions to align with the new position without upsetting my existing team (an example of a mentor-based activity). Then when meeting with a few key executives, he made the time to share why my contributions in this new team would benefit the company (an example of a sponsor-based activity). Once I had executive buy-in, my team leader seemed more willing to accept and support my professional desires to join this new team.

Advisory Boards. An ensemble made up of those in your inner circle upon whom you call for advice, guidance and elevation. These are often a gathering of coaches, mentors and sponsors that can change over time.

CHAPTER FOURTEEN

Identifying, Joining and Participating on Boards

Many times throughout this book, I mention boards of directors. These bodies are typically made up of people who are not directly affiliated with the company, but who are willing to commit a portion of their time and energy to helping the company maximize its potential. Some boards elect members; others appoint them and then oversee the activities of that organization. Regardless of where you are in your career journey, pursuing a board of director's seat for-profit or non-for-profit organizations could be advantageous to your professional development, network and future trajectory. In fact, I have seen many women gain additional leadership skills and experience while advancing their professional brand through these types of opportunities.

Some women, based on their network, experience and results are directly invited to join the board, but this is not the case for all women. Many start in a committee or project-based role before a board invitation is extended. Depending on your available time and existing network, it may make sense to start by participating in a related committee or project first. This will often give you insider insight to better understand the inner workings of the organization and, if desired, help determine the path for a future board seat.

What I have learned is that there are no hard and fast rules or a specific playbook to landing a board seat. In fact, I was surprised to learn through an informal request to women within my LinkedIn network, that there are many avenues to gain and expand these professional experiences.

I could provide a list of activities, ideas and suggestions based on my experiences to help you position yourself for a future board seat, but as I do with many endeavors, I find multiple people who have related experiences and ask about their processes. Each woman below has held at least one board seat. I have asked them to share their paths and some of the insights they have gained along the way.

Amy Franko
Founder and President
Impact Instruction Group
What board(s) are you on or have you been on?
Girl Scouts of Ohio's Heartland, member at large, chair of the board development committee.

How did you get invited to join the board?
I was invited by the CEO and board chair. I began in a committee role on the board development committee that grew into a member at large role and committee chair.

Did you need a sponsor, someone to help you connect to the right people or someone who nominated you?
In this case, the CEO and board chair were my sponsors. I did have to apply for the role, and go through an interview/vetting process. The board slate is approved by council delegates at the annual meeting each year.

Why did you want to join this board?
First and foremost, I am passionate about the cause of girls and leadership. The Girl Scouts is one of the most recognizable brands and premier leadership development organizations in the country. I knew I could make a difference, apply my skills and learn new skills, as well as interact with community and business leaders.

Does being on the board help your career path?
I believe it does. I've had the opportunity to interact with community and business leaders and build relationships I may not otherwise have had the opportunity to do. Chairing board development directly correlates to my business, Impact Instruction Group in leadership development. I have a future goal of corporate board service, and I know these experiences will be extremely valuable.

Anonymous Nonprofit Executive
Board Chair
Women Business Center
What board(s) are you on or have you been on?
I have been a on few boards in the past that were in conjunction with my full-time role. As a part of the executive team of a nonprofit that funded nonprofits and entrepreneurs, part of our role was to participate on the boards of organizations we funded. Now pursuing new endeavors, I recently joined the Women Business Center of NEO board as an advisory board chair, which is outside of my work-based initiatives. I am passionate to help grow the organization and positively impact the businesswomen in my community.

How did you get invited to join the board?
Based on my results in previous roles and community initiatives, I was asked by the executive director of the WBC to join their board as the board chair.

Did you need a sponsor, someone to help you connect to the right people or someone who nominated you?
For this specific invitation, no. I have worked on my professional brand and network for decades, and the WBC advisory board chair opportunity found me.

Does being on the board help your career path?
I have not actively pursued board memberships mostly because of the time commitment. I made a decision to put all of my free non-working time into being with my children. This strategy has not hurt my career because I was involved in many initiatives through my full-time position that helped pave my professional path. Now that my children are older and my executive focus has again transformed, I have more time to select boards that I am drawn to advancing their mission.

Susan Luria
Health Care Executive
What board(s) are you on or have you been on?
Current boards: One early stage company and one educational institution.
Past boards: Multiple early stage company and nonprofit boards.

How did you get invited to join the board?

The path to each of the boards was different, but all came from developing and maintaining strong relationships with people over many years.

What prompted these board invitations?

For the early stage companies, I served as an active supporter or connector to resources (money, team, customers) for the entrepreneur leaders. Each of the civic board invitations came from some level of involvement—participant, volunteer, member—with the organization. I like to ask a lot of questions and learn a lot about the people and organizations with which I work. Doing so leads to a deeper level involvement than passive participant with a natural next step being direct involvement as a board member or adviser.

What lessons have you learned?

Boards need a variety of skills and backgrounds. It can take time to align your interest and their needs.

Don't be afraid to target the organizations that inspire you and articulate your interest and passion. I served in a variety of volunteer positions for more than 10 years for my alma mater without actually telling anybody that my true passion was to serve on a particular Board of Visitors. I finally wrote a letter to multiple leaders of the organization expressing my interest, passion and desire to serve in a particular role—and my interest was a surprise to all of them. It took two years before a position opened on that Board of Visitors for me, but I ended up where I wanted to be. Don't be afraid to let people know where you want to serve—and don't be afraid of rejection. You may not be asked because they simply may have too many people with your skill set or background engaged already.

I think it is important to share that I have also ended up leaving two boards before my term officially ended. I hope I did so gracefully and helped recruit others to fill my term, but it still caused me much consternation. What I learned from this is that boards are great if they fit your interest and/or career passion, but to do it right you need to have the combination of time and passion for the organization and its mission. Both boards I left early took a significant amount of time. At that point in my life, I could not justify focusing my time on these boards as they were both unrelated to my current job and my personal long-term interests and passion. I realized that time is a currency I have to protect—saying yes to something (a board position) also means saying no to something I may want to prioritize (time with my daughters).

Nicole Hayward
CMO, OnSIP
Board Member and Technology Chair, Women in the Channel
What board(s) are you on or have you been on?

I am on the board of Women in the Channel, a professional nonprofit supporting women in leadership roles in the channel sector of the telecom and data industry. We come together because as the industry grows, changes and expands the number of female leaders at top levels shrinks.

How did you get invited to join the board?

I was invited to join the board through my volunteerism. I joined the organization and offered my marketing technology experience, building a new website and selecting cloud platforms to run our organization. I quickly became chair of the web committee, a proven path to the board as it showcases one's dedication and leadership skills. With my finger on the pulse of operations, I was invited to apply to the board within a year's time.

Does being on the board help your career path?

Being on the board for a nonprofit in my industry has elevated both my personal brand and the brand of my current organization. I regularly collaborate with the industry's top leaders, which has resulted in new business partnerships and a strong professional network. For example, as a board member, I was just asked to give a short speech to a sold-out industry event—providing me exposure that money could not buy, but volunteering my time and energy has provided those benefits and much more.

Janet Meeks
Co-founder and CEO
Healthcare Alignment Advisors LLC
What board(s) are you on or have you been on?

Thirty-One Gifts LLC, Columbus, Ohio ($700 million privately held company), advisory board member October 2012 to present (appointed when advisory board was formed in October 2012, currently serving a second term); Rev1 Ventures: Westerville First Connect, Westerville, Ohio, advisory board responsible for assessing emerging technologies from startup corporations, 2013 to 2015; Eye Center of Columbus, Columbus, Ohio (for-profit syndicated joint venture Ambulatory Surgery Center), board of directors, 2008 to 2013; Vanderbilt University Medical Center, Nashville, Tennessee, Concentra/Vanderbilt LLC, *board of governors, 1999 to 2002; Community Health Consortium, board of directors, 1998 to 2002, secretary, 1998 to 2000 and vice president, 2000 to 2002.*

How did you get invited?
For the Thirty-One Gifts advisory board, I was invited by the founder and CEO following an interview. For several of the other boards, I was approached by the CEO or another C-suite executive. Most of the work-related boards were appointments made by the CEO.

Did you need a sponsor, someone to help you connect to the right people or someone who nominated you?
While sponsorship is critically important, most of my appointments have been through people with whom I have served previously and/or who were familiar with my work, particularly as I served as a hospital president and COO for nine years. In the case of Thirty-One Gifts, I had met one of their executives who had recommended me.

Why did you want to join this board?
I believe in the importance of matching the passion of the person with the purpose of the work. Thirty-One Gifts exists to encourage, to celebrate and to reward women. This purpose resonated with my personal calling to help others become all they are created to be.

Does being on the board help your career path?
Yes. Through my service with Thirty-One Gifts' advisory board, in particular, this set me on fire to seek to serve on the fiduciary boards of publicly held or substantive, privately held companies.

Andrea Knapp
Scientific Professional, Chapter Chair President and Board Member
Women in Bio
What is your board experience?
My board experience has been on a volunteer basis for nonprofit volunteer or professional organizations. I am currently on and have been on the board for Women In Bio (Seattle Metro) since 2013.

How did you get invited to join the board?
As all of my positions have been volunteer based, I have come into my positions based on degree of involvement with the organizations and either volunteered or been asked to throw my name into the hat for a

role. *Most recently with Women In Bio, I simply told the then current leadership that I wanted to be the next president-elect.*

Did you need a sponsor, someone to help you connect to the right people or someone who nominated you?
I've never needed a sponsor, but found that taking the time to talk with people currently or previously in positions of interest to me to get a better idea of what to expect and what is needed proved very helpful.

Why did you want to join this board?
All the boards I have been a part of were out of a desire to impact that organization. Leadership provides the opportunity to sit at the table that is making decisions and steering the ship.

Does being on the board help your career path?
Even though my board involvement has been volunteer based, it has a tremendous impact on my career. Most notably it provides leadership experience when it may not otherwise be readily available in my current job. Currently, I am leading a board of 15 with a membership of just under 200. While I was the training chair for Junior League last year, I led a committee training for more than 700 members with the help of 25 volunteers over 30 sessions. After moving to a new city where I knew no one, involvement at this level has also helped me grow out of a painful shyness I experienced as a kid, to meet new people and grow and develop as a leader.

Jackie Adams, an engineer and nonprofit leader, answered the question, "Does being on the board help your career path?" with, "I believe serving on the board helps add to my credibility as a nonprofit leader. It's also given me insights on how a well-run organization functions and provided great networking connections."

I truly appreciate all the women who contributed their firsthand insight that demonstrates to me—and I am sure to many of you—there are no perfect paths or exact time in your career or methods of how or when you should pursue a board seat.

As I think about my professional journey, I have to admit that I did not believe I was ready for a board seat when it appeared, but after I was part of the board, I recognized that I was ready and I had something to offer and gain. I have had to learn to appreciate where I have been and where I am going and not sell myself short on what is possible now.

As I reflect on the insight above and my own board's journey, I too was invited because of my work and outcomes in the technology industry. The executive director, whom I had known for years, contacted me as the board was looking for more technology focused members as well as additional diverse professionals.

Many of the insights stated above are themes throughout this book. Things to keep in minds as you approach new endeavors:
- Deliver results in your existing roles and projects.
- Invest in your network as they will often be instrumental in your journey.
- Share your accomplishments with others.
- Be a resource for others.
- Let your desires be known.

As you think about the women and their fabulous contributions above, what resonates with you based on where you are now in your professional journey? Take a few moments to jot down some of your key takeaways from this chapter.

Some of my takeaways are:
- Be honest with how much time you have and how much you want to contribute to meaningful initiatives. What I have learned is there is time for most goals, but often they have their place in your career and life journey. Some of us can juggle many things, and others want more quality time focused on fewer things at one time. The great thing is, you get to decide when it is right to explore additional opportunities such as a board seat.
- These commitments can enhance your professional brand, but they often require a commitment. Be responsible for the commitments you make to serve on boards. These companies are looking to you for your experience, your expertise and your perspective. If you offer your services, you need to follow through with active participation as many are depending on you. If you're limited in time, but still want to help, make that clear from the beginning. A common rule of thumb I follow: It's better to under promise and over deliver than the alternative.
- Being part of a board of directors can often create an opportunity to interact with community and business leaders that might otherwise be difficult to connect and network with based on your day job.

- Jumping directly into your desired board seat may happen, but if not, consider joining a committee to prove your value, gain insider insight into the inner workings of the board and identify sponsors to help pave your path toward a future board seat.
- Your career and life likely have twists and turns, and you may encounter a time where you need to change directions and change boards. Alignments, including board seats, are often instruments when working to catapult toward your desired goals.
- External involvement such as committee member, chair or board member can provide leadership experience when it may not otherwise be readily available in my current job.
- Be sure to let your desires be known, ask for the role you desire, especially when you have a track record of results.

It has become evident to me that there is rarely one event, one person or one action that catapults you in the direction of your life purpose; it is more often a series of decisions, actions and connections each day that creates the momentum for you to leap.

CHAPTER FIFTEEN

Maneuvering Cultures

A s you identify ways to create more relevance, you may recognize that you need to create more ways to elevate your work, accomplishments and professional goals. Through this process, you may realize that your professional situation is hindering your ability to receive the recognition, sponsorship and elevation needed to accelerate your influence and impact.

I want to discuss bosses, fear and getting out of your comfort zone. But before I do, let's quickly look at a few things that make professional women successful.

A recent post on CAREEREALISM titled "5 Things Possessed By Successful Women In IT" has an interesting, and likely true tag line: "Every Job is Temporary," highlighting the great inclusion and diversity initiatives within the Amtrak organization. The article states:

> *It takes a few key traits to be considered for these roles at any company. This is particularly true with a business like Amtrak that is recognized as a STEM Job Employer for encouraging workforce diversity and aligning careers with STEM education programs.*

The articles' list of five things applies to most professionals:
• Skill
• Curiosity
• Ambition
• Passion
• Team

I like this list because it highlights many of the things we have already discussed in some fashion, and it ends with team. You can generally control the first four items on this list, but the last item is dependent on you and your interactions with others.

Within my work, many great professional women shared their excitements and discouragements within their work environments. There are numerous reasons why a woman is not motivated and engaged at work and I'm sure you can even think of a few more than I have.

It seems in addition to your direct manager, the company's culture is important. It may be argued based on many data points that women put more value on a productive culture than men. Hewlett and Marshall's executive summary, "Women Want Five Things" states:

> *This report examines the flywheels of women's fierce ambition: What drives them, what inspires them to remain fully engaged and on track for leadership roles. They find that across geographies, well-qualified women have a five-point value proposition.*

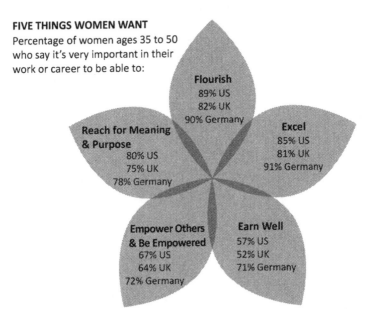

FIVE THINGS WOMEN WANT
Percentage of women ages 35 to 50 who say it's very important in their work or career to be able to:

Flourish
89% US
82% UK
90% Germany

Reach for Meaning & Purpose
80% US
75% UK
78% Germany

Excel
85% US
81% UK
91% Germany

Empower Others & Be Empowered
67% US
64% UK
72% Germany

Earn Well
57% US
52% UK
71% Germany

Source: Sylvia Ann Hewlett and Melinda Marshall. "Women Want Five Things." The Center for Talent and Innovation: Dec. 9, 2014.

I share this with executives—along with other studies—that are looking to recruit and retain experienced women in technology and related fields. Many of these executives spend hours reviewing and discussing the importance and difference of how women and men engage in the workplace.

As many of us know firsthand, technology-based environments and related fields that align with STEM are known to foster some interesting cultures that often do not align with some of the cultural characteristics women seek at work.

Many of these same environments breed unhealthy work situations that can be contained to one team or leader, but may taint an entire organization.

Jasmine Tsai's post hit home for me because it focused on cultures where it is difficult to pinpoint the exact culprit, yet the culture is a true energy drainer that often creates career potholes forcing good people into other industries or leaving the workforce altogether. Tsai's 2014 article "Stopping Toxicity in Your Engineering Culture" states:

> *It is not to say it's always easy to stand up against them, especially if you are in an organization that is poorly managed and riddled with fundamentally misaligned beliefs.*

Like many, I have been engulfed in these rubbish cultures where you cannot get out soon enough and the whole team suffers. When it happens, I am so disappointed that I ended up in this situation and frustrated that I need to find ways to help fix the culture or create paths to new cultures.

Now, before I jump haphazardly into a new job, board seat or initiatives, it's often helpful to consider a few lessons learned so I don't land in an environment that fosters negative results for the team, the project or me. First, I step back from the emotion of the situation and look for the lessons I can learn. I have taken many lessons away from unfortunate situations.

Think for a few minutes about a time you were in a situation that you were eager to escape. What made this situation uncomfortable and undesirable? Was it a person, a boss, a group of people, deadlines, the product or project? Was it personality types, unrealistic expectations, power struggles, too many egos involved or other characteristics that drove you away? Were there inconsistencies in internal or external goals or a lack of decision-making abilities? Was it the way people communicated with you or their lack of communication?

The chart below helps me capture—at a high level—what I need and what I need to avoid:

Cultures I Thrive In	Traits of Leaders I Aspire to Work For	Characteristics of Cultures I Must Avoid

Think back to the last 10 years. Where have you excelled and where have you needed to jump? What were the traits of the leaders that effectively motivated you to succeed? What were the triggers that you will work to avoid or dodge in the future? Having insight as to what type of leader, culture and environment works best for you can be quite useful as you learn about new ways to accelerate.

I often use this chart when women are looking to expand in new directions. It is critical, as we get more experienced in our career, that we interview others as they are interviewing us. Knowing what works for you is important, but aligning those to new opportunities is key. We can do this by asking good questions based on the chart above.

For example, if you're more productive with high-level managers that let you run with projects, be sure you ask about this as you look at new initiatives. If you like offices with flex start and end times because you can do work anywhere, be sure to ask about this. Many women are still apprehensive to ask too many pointed questions during the interview phase.

UNMOTIVATED

Unmotivated by your environment, work or team? Do you feel like you are not challenged? If so, these are important things your boss and leaders should know. I suggest not just going into these conversations with problems, but leveraging the problem to showcase ideas of where you might engage in new levels to add more value.

Your leadership team is likely interested in good ideas. I can assure you that attrition is a big issue for a lot of organizations. In many situations, it can be a direct correlation to the project you are assigned that could be pushing you to stay or leave.

Hewlett, in her 2014 *Harvard Business Review* article titled "What's Holding Women Back in Science and Technology Industries," shares an insightful graph:

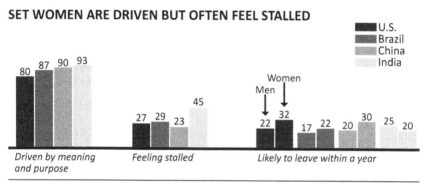

SET WOMEN ARE DRIVEN BUT OFTEN FEEL STALLED

Source: Sylvia Ann Hewlett. "What's Holding Women Back in Science and Technology Industries." Harvard Business Review: March 13, 2014.

If you are feeling unmotivated, unengaged and/or not aligned with the right things, be professional and schedule a meetings with people who can help address the issues, solve your hurdles or alter your path. As I mentioned above, bring your concerns and issues, but also bring suggestions. I find many leaders are overworked too and don't always have the time or energy to check in as much as needed with their team members. I can assure you, they would rather work to get you to stay than to find new people to replace you. Recruiting new talent is not only expensive, but also time-consuming and the ramp-up time can impact key deadlines.

If you have already scheduled the meetings, worked with the right people and are still feeling misaligned, you may want to read a great piece on The Glasshammer by Robin Madell called "Should I Stay or Should I Go?" Madell integrates great studies and bullets on how to go about making decisions beyond your gut, which she refers to as "data-driven evaluations." I am a big fan of data-based decisions, as I like to do my research before making big decisions. Among other great advice, Madell shares the pitfalls we may encounter if we base our decisions on assumptions.

It is important to keep your eye on the ball, even if you are in one of these tough cultures or feeling misaligned with your work. No matter how bad it gets, be sure you work to protect your reputation and brand, even in the most challenging of environments. It is unlikely people will remember the culture or environment, but they will remember how you reacted.

Be careful not to burn bridges or harm any relationships you may have developed over the years. These people are part of your network and may become important in a different capacity in years to come. A list you surely want to avoid is outlined in Bill Murphy Jr.'s "10 Bad Habits That Make You Look Really Unprofessional."

Take the time to recognize the decisions that may be slotting you into these undesirable cultures and teams. This is especially important to be aware of when you are looking to jump in a new direction, as I am sure you are not looking for a repeat performance. Before jumping, meet with people who can help address the issues, solve your hurdles or alter your path with your existing company.

It takes time to find new opportunities and I know firsthand, many companies and leader would rather help you work through a situation or into a new group than have you move on to another organization.

In both outcomes, identifying cultures you thrive in, leaders you aspire to work for and culture traits you want to avoid are important and worth doing before engaging mentors and sponsors to help you accelerate your path.

CHAPTER SIXTEEN

Aligning With Impactful Work

It is important to mention again that not all professionals desire to advance in an organization. Many professional women I have met along the way are looking to expand their influence in their existing teams, or to add external initiatives to enhance their areas of impact such as committees, boards, new programs or activities.

In a 2015 *Bloomberg Business* article by Rebecca Greenfield, titled "One Reason Women Aren't Getting the Promotion: They Don't Want It," Greenfield shares a viewpoint that might not be a surprise to professional women:

> *Women are underrepresented in leadership positions for plenty of reasons: They're stereotyped as being less competent than men, they aren't as aggressive, and there's a perception that they can't lead and raise a family at the same time. Now, research from Harvard Business School adds yet another reason to the list: Women aren't in leadership positions because they just don't want the jobs as much as men do.*

Now you may or may not agree with the statement above as it relates to you and your professional goals. But I wanted to include this perspective because I know many women who have declined promotions. Some have personally decided that they want their job only to occupy a certain percentage of their life. The belief is that additional responsibility, or new opportunities will alter the imprint their job, and the related responsibilities, plays in their lives. Others are very satisfied with their current position and some enjoy working with a specific manager and team.

Regardless of the reason, this is a personal decision and knowing yourself and your life goals is what truly matters. How you get there is up to you. Your choices should reflect the approach you are taking to manifest your life goals.

With this, I am fully aware that not all women want to move up in their career. Some prefer to zigzag into interesting positions or to work for specific leaders or initiatives. There is no right approach. Knowing who you are and what you desire is most important, especially if you are not being controlled by fear, assumptions and unjustified barriers.

One thing I will add is that many women assume moving up means more hours. In fact, I just spoke at a large technology conference and during the question and answer portion of the keynote, a woman in tech with 18 years of experience shared that she recently declined a promotion. I asked her why. I had no expectations or delayed judgment; I was truly interested in her perspective and route to that decision.

She said, "I didn't feel ready, and I couldn't handle any more hours at work."

I was disheartened by her response, but recognize that this is happening every day in companies around the nation. Women are declining new opportunities for a variety of reasons including assumptions, workload and team culture. For those of you reading this book in order, you likely see some glimpses of self-sabotage in her answer too, which we discussed as self-doubt in previous chapters.

Her comment brought me back to something I read a few years ago. It was an awakening as I read it then and as I reflected on my career. I felt it was also applicable to this situation.

When I was reading Lois P. Frankel's best-seller *Nice Girls Don't Get the Corner Office: 101 Unconscious Mistakes Women Make That Sabotage Their Careers*, I remember pausing many times to mentally digest Frankel's relevant and meaningful professional advice. I reflected again on this book when this woman shared her concerns.

One of my personal takeaways from reading this book was that moving up in the organization may not equate to more work hours. Taking on more leadership roles may mean strategically leading more people to get the right work done.

A great glimpse into this book is shared in an online interview posted on Women for Hire, where Frankel is asked five questions.

If you spend time reviewing Frankel's insight, I bet you too will gain many professional nuggets.

THE WORK

Since we are talking about work, let's spend some time talking about how you decide which projects make sense for you based on where you are and what you want to impact in the future. Have you ever thought about how you align yourself with the right work?

If you are thinking, "What do you mean, I have a job, and they give me projects." There may be some investigating to do in your "yeses." Now, I am not suggesting that you just start declining work. But I do suggest you spend some time to better understand how projects are distributed among and across your team.

I find when I share the "Power of No" chart (**Chapter 7: Targeting Your Relevance to Enrich Your Brand**) during my consulting and keynote work, many women take on new projects regularly without inquiring more about the expected results, direct impact, allocated budget or other key criteria. If you are a person who delivers great results, I am sure you too are asked to take on many projects inside and outside of work.

Now, in your 20s, you often cannot be picky about the work you are assigned because you are working to build a track record of results, which often drives future career opportunities. As you move along into your 30s and beyond, aligning with the right work can be essential to your career trajectory.

Take a look at this eye-opening research addressing "the work" and "project assignments" included in a 2013 *Harvard Business Review* article titled "Women in the Workplace: A Research Roundup:"

> • *Men get more of the critical assignments that lead to advancement than women do, according to a recent Catalyst study of 1,660 business school graduates, which examined the nature of projects given to high-potential employees.*
> • *On average the men's projects had budgets twice as big and had three times as many staffers as the women's.*
> • *Only 22 percent of the women, but 30 percent of the men, were given budgets of more than $10 million, and just 46 percent of the women, versus 56 percent of the*

> *men, received P&L responsibility.*
> - *Even more telling, while more than a third of the men reported that their assignments garnered them a great deal of attention from the C-suite, only about a quarter of the women could say the same.*

I ask you now, do you think the work assigned to you matters? I have to admit I might have been naive in assuming that many managers were dividing the work and opportunity fairly based on skill set, potential and future opportunities. Now looking back maybe they did, maybe they did not.

I am not pointing fingers. I will even suggest that I am responsible because I do not recall a time during my first 15 years where I questioned the work assigned to me. I also did not assume that others received more plum projects. After seeing these data points, however, I am much more inquisitive and aware of how and what work is distributed.

Now, I am not suggesting that you go into work with blazing requests or assumptions because not all work environments are the same. I am suggesting you add this to your bag of professional awareness and knowledge and use it wisely. A good time to discuss project allocation is during your annual review, when accepting new positions and when asked, "What do you want to do next?"

When assigned new work, be sure you ask some of these questions from my e-book, *Before You Say Yes*:
- What are the expected results of this project?
- What is the timeline?
- Who is already involved in this project?
- What are the interdependencies of this work within the organization?
- What is the budget?
- What known obstacles exist?
- Why is this project important to the company?
- What if this does not get done within the expected timeline and budget?

There are many more questions you can ask based on your knowledge of the company, previous projects and dependencies. But this will at least get you thinking about what to investigate before you jump in and say, "Sure, I'll work on that project, too."

Since many of us have multiple projects at any one time, it is not critical to have all stellar or priority one projects at once. In fact, it could be very difficult to deliver your best results if all your projects were all high-priority, high visibility. I find I am most effective when I have a mix of projects with various milestone dates so I am not running full speed all the time. I strive for a flow in deliverables and visibility.

With this, I leverage the chart below to understand my different projects based on specific characteristics. This chart, which started on a whiteboard, allows me to see the major projects I have underway with the key milestones, exposure and impact. This chart may also help you gain additional insight as it relates to your current projects:

	Project A	Project B
Alignment to Your Current or Future Goals		
Impact to the Company (Revenue/Operations/Brand)		
Benefit to Your Customers		
Executive Visibility		
Profit & Loss Responsibility		
Professional Growth Opportunity		
Professional Fulfillment		
Timeline (Milestones by Date)		

You could also use this chart, with some additional rows—Project Effectiveness, Unexpected Outcomes, Level of Impact—to assess how previous projects have served you. I have found that sometimes my expectations when starting a project are not aligned with the outcomes. Reflecting back on these projects provides me addition insight. Through this reflection I have found that I should spend more time upfront understanding the desired outcomes, potential obstacles and other people or groups that could be instrumental to the project's progression.

Remember as you update your LinkedIn profile and resume to transfer specific details included here, as it relates to current and previous projects, to those professional overviews of your work. When applicable, highlight measurable metrics that are often clear indications of your previous areas of impact and related accomplishments.

Understanding the work assigned to you, how it fits into the company's goals and how it can position you, your skills and relevance for where you want to accelerate your impact next are important. Project assignment can be a critical piece of your professional brand and future path.

Be aware of how your projects align with both the company's goals and your goals by completing each section of the chart based on the projects you are assigned. Note, depending on your role in each project, your categorizations may change.

For example, if you are leading the project you will have more details than you would have if you are only working on a small piece of it. If you have 10 projects, and you only have a slice of work on each, it might be time to consider positioning yourself for a larger role on fewer projects.

Hopefully you can leverage this information in your professional sphere to be more proactive as it relates to aligning with particular work assignments. Spend some time thinking about how you position yourself for future projects that can showcase your ability, attitude and value based on where you desire to accelerate your impact. It is likely others will guide you along the way, but you do need to drive your career in the direction you desire.

CHAPTER SEVENTEEN

Exploring Lateral Moves

I became familiar with the phrase "climbing the corporate ladder" during college, which was more than 20 years ago. The phrases "going up," "executive leadership" and "breaking through to the top" seemed to be reinforced in the earlier years of my career as the desired path for all. Like a ladder, the path appeared to be an upward movement from an entry-level position toward the positions of power and leadership.

With more experience and perspective, there does not seem to be just one ladder or just one way to use it. In fact, Sheryl Sandberg believes we should consider our career path more as a jungle gym. In a 2013 *Forbes* article titled "Sheryl Sandberg's 5 Best 'Lean In' Tips For Women," Kerry Hannon shares her favorite tips that she learned from Sandberg:

> *'Visualize your career as a jungle gym, not a ladder.' This is my favorite of Sandberg's tips. (Maybe that's because when I was growing up, I loved playing on the jungle gym in our backyard.) She attributes the analogy to* Fortune *editor-at-large Patricia Sellers, who heads up the magazine's 'Most Powerful Women' franchise. To me, it's a great image of the 21st-century career path.*
>
> *'Ladders are limiting,' Sandberg writes. 'Jungle gyms offer more creative exploration. There are many ways to get to the top of a jungle gym. The ability to forge a unique path with occasional dips, detours, and even dead ends presents a better chance for fulfillment'*

I love this visual, especially as I reflect on my career, which seems more like a climbing wall. Think about the climbing walls you often see at the sporting goods stores. You must be in good shape, show up with the right tools and look for small advancements to make your way to your desired platform.

From my perspective, some of those openings will be clear such as promotions or a new department lead while others may be more defined as sidesteps that can show up as projects, mentoring opportunities or cross-departmental training. In some cases, you may or may not have a sponsor pulling the strings for you to gain the momentum you need to leap toward that next critical step, even if it seems to be a lateral move.

In *Next Avenue*'s 2012 article, "Your Next Job Could Be a Lateral Move—on Your Way to the Top," Joanne Cleaver teaches us more about the value of the ever-changing organizational structures as Laurie Nordholt, of Time Warner Cable, shares her experience:

> *When Time Warner Cable condensed its traditional, multilevel management structure into fewer, more powerful positions, she catapulted from a regional sales vice president in charge of one state to a regional sales vice president heading up several. Nordholt's title didn't change, but her responsibilities certainly did. That was her light-bulb moment. 'I realized that to continue to be successful, you have to be extremely nimble and help lead change,' Nordholt says. So from then on, Nordholt determined that her success would be marked not by her title, but by her personal reputation and influence.*

Whether it is title, location or team, sometimes the value to our careers seem insignificant if it is associated with a lateral move, but you may want to reconsider this viewpoint.

Salary.com offers "14 Reasons to Consider a Lateral Move," including some of my favorites:

- *Reason No. 1: You want to enhance your value and be more marketable.*
- *Reason No. 3: You want more visibility.*
- *Reason No. 6: You want to build your network within the company.*

- *Reason No. 7: You are burnt out, and want to revitalize.*
- *Reason No. 9: You want to break out of a stagnant situation.*
- *Reason No. 12: You want to better match your values with that of the department or organization.*

I suggest you check out the other great reasons that complete this list as well as other articles by author Dawn Dugan.

If you feel that you can connect with No. 7 or No. 9 because your current role is leaving you unmotivated or you have the weekly Sunday Night Blues, as stated in the 2015 Huffington Post article by Caroline Dowd-Higgins titled "How To Recharge, Reignite or Reinvent Your Career," it may be time to find ways to stir the career pot to generate new energies, opportunities and excitement.

Even if you do not have the blues, be sure you are not settling too long in a position. If you are going to a job where "your wisdom is not welcome, there are no hills to climb, and there is no one to learn from," as Liz Ryan states in her 2015 *Forbes* article "Five Signs Your Job Is Holding You Back," it may be time to stretch in new directions.

I know it can be scary and you may even say I am not ready or qualified for many of the open positions, but it is likely others are not either. I bet you know how to solve problems, find people to help and prioritize what matters with your direct manager, which of course is not all you need to be successful. But these qualities get you moving in the right direction.

Staying in roles where you are unchallenged and overqualified is surely not a stretch.

In a 2014 *Fortune* article, "How to Stay Excited About Your Career? Never Take a Job You're Qualified For," Liz Wiseman, president of the Wiseman Group, shares some of her advice on stretch positions:

- *Take a job in a new domain.*
- *Take on a stretch challenge.*
- *Take on a broader role.*
- *Borrow a job.*

I like Wiseman's list and appreciate her final thoughts as she closes out the article and states:

> *What if someone isn't willing to take a chance on you? Then this might be one of those occasions when it's best just to show up for the party rather than wait for an invitation. Don't unilaterally seize control of a bigger job, but do take the initiative to work beyond the scope of your current job. Ask your manager what work you can take off her plate. Start small and prove yourself.*

As you investigate ways to move through your career, resist the urge only to look up. A new opportunity, even if it's not a promotion from your current role, could be very rewarding. Be sure to examine what you might be able to contribute to, learn by participating in or who you might meet along the way.

As you find these new opportunities, it is likely they will want to know more about you, even if you are inquiring informally. As I share with many women, it often takes nine to 12 months to cultivate the right move, which is unfortunate for many women since they often come to me when they are on their last thread. If you think a change is on your horizon, start researching some stretch positions now as a potential place to land next. I even suggest swapping roles with another person in your organization as Wiseman suggests in her list.

As you start exploring—even through informal activity—it is likely people will investigate you both online and in-person. So be sure you have taken the time to manicure your online presence. If you are getting more serious about your research and interest in potential opportunities, it is a good time to ask yourself some of these questions:

- When is the last time I updated my resume?
- Do my resume highlight measure milestones, key projects and delivered outcomes?
- Do I need help with my resume?
- How would I rate my LinkedIn profile?
- Does my resume and LinkedIn profile echo each other?
- Do I have references within my profile that can speak to my work?
- Who in my network can help me align with these new areas of interest?

Through these activities, related research opportunities and new conversations, many women realize that they need to align their professional brand to reflect where they have been and where they plan to accelerate their impact, especially as they are looking to stretch in new directions.

This realization is common for many professionals as they prepare for what is next. Professional positioning and related branding are critical steps to land in these stretch roles. Some people can package and position their work, and others leverage professional resources such as coaches, online experts and resume writers for help. Depending on your skills, expertise and timeline, it might be beneficial to invest in these resources. It has helped me on numerous occasions.

As we discussed in previous chapters, enhancing your relevance, nurturing connections, effectively representing your accomplishments, communicating your desired direction and maneuvering the professional landscape are all important well before you are ready to jump toward new roles and responsibilities.

CHAPTER EIGHTEEN

Maximizing Risk and Minimizing Fears

I cannot tell you how many emails and calls I get each month where women make assumptions about what is or is not possible. I am often surprised how quickly they jump to "I am not ready for that" or "I do not have that type of training" or "My company would never give me that opportunity." I often ask them questions that have some flavor of:

- Did someone notable tell you "no"?
- Even if it was "no" and from a notable source, are they the only option?
- Have you taken the time to research your options?
- Who can help you pave the way?

I am not sure I have always had this much grit, but over the last two decades, I think I have built up my risk-taking muscle. This term is included in Meg Duffy's article and seems to pop up fairly often in my line of sight. You may think risk-taking is a trait, but I think it is a learned behavior built from small actions that push your boundaries. These small wins that exercise your risk muscle can eventually increase your ability to ask for more, apply when you are not 100 percent ready and raise your hand when you are reluctant to do so.

> In their groundbreaking 2014 article and book The Confidence Gap, Katty Kay and Claire Shipman outlined the genetic predispositions and environmental factors that contribute to confidence. And, as part of their research, Kay and Shipman found that women take significantly fewer risks than men, leading to lower confidence levels which can stifle career growth.

Duffy outlines in "3 Steps For Bridging 'The Confidence Gap'" some excellent steps including, "No. 2: Discover Your Risk-Taking Muscles," where she describes the step with effective details.

Here is the section that resonated with me:

> *The experimentation process is meant to be uncomfortable because it forces you to acknowledge your fears and push ahead. If you analyze an opportunity, and your hang-ups may include 'I'm afraid,' or 'I don't know' which is okay. It means it's a great time to do it and find out. Because a risk can be as small as an email, you can chip away at your goals and make progress every day.*

Assuming you can or assuming you cannot is likely foreshadowing your future state. With these additional insights based on research, hopefully, you will not jump into assumptions about what is possible for you, but rather make informed decisions based on those insights.

FEAR

Fear, unfortunately, is a huge obstacle for professional women—it can show up in many forms throughout your day and in many cases, impact your decisions, direction and eventually your impact. Carol Sankar asks in her 2015 LinkedIn post "Shattering the 'Glass Ceiling' Mindset:"

> *Is it the actual fear of rejection or the lack of confidence to approach the opportunity that is impacting the way women approach their success?*

Now that you have additional perspective based on the articles and strategies in this book, let's spend a few minutes thinking about how fear has impacted your decisions, by using the chart on the next page.

The chart on the next page ends with the last scenario because, in the middle of Sankar's post, she highlights a study that echoes our fear of connecting with people we do not know:

> *Then, there is the fear of the unknown for women. In a recent study we conducted with 100 subjects in our consultancy, 71 percent of the respondents said that they are intimidated to contact prospects and leaders on their own.*

	Yes, Fear Held Me Back	I Was Fearful, But Pushed Forward
I often have important pieces of data to contribute to the group, but have been interrupted so many times that I am not sure my input is necessary or appreciated.		
A position was posted that I was interested in, but I did not think I would be considered.		
My boss told me I was not ready to move out of my current role. I wanted to share interest in potential promotions with other key people in my organization to nurture sponsorships outside of my direct team.		
I accept more of the administrative tasks because that is often what is asked of me within my team, even though I aspire for more meaningful and technically based work.		
My ideas have been overlooked in past meetings; I do not want to offer up other ideas for fear of _____.		
I am getting older, so I work to stay under the radar most of the time and just do my work even though I see jobs I would like to move into next.		
I have been asked to present at meetings or conferences, but I think others will do a better job.		
When asked my opinion, I think I should keep it brief because others often look disinterested in my input.		
I have opportunities to speak to key executives, but I often struggle on what to say, so I consider avoiding these encounters.		

Another article by Madell titled "Overcome Fears to Do Better at Work" in *U.S. News & World Report* has great action-based advice from Gail Sheehy, author of 17 books, including the best-selling classic *Passages*, and her recent memoir, *Daring: My Passages*.

She highlights "the five secrets to conquering doubt and achieving your full potential." It is a great list of five points, and I particularly love, "No. 5: Learn to swap fear for daring." Sure it is a bit of a mind trick, but when I cannot get enough self-assurance to move forward it often seems to do the trick to push me forward. Madell goes on to say:

> *While Sheehy admits she hasn't been fearless in every challenging situation and has seldom met women who have...she developed a habit that, when she felt fear, she would dare herself to push through it and do what needed to be done.*
>
> *'To dare risk jumping out of your comfort zone changes the way people respond to you,' Sheehy says. 'That changes the way you see yourself. Even when I didn't land on my feet at first—which was often—I learned something useful and dared to try again. The only way out of fear is through.'*

Through my stretch situations, where I have pushed through fear or actively practiced my risk muscle or both, I too have come to appreciate where career pitfalls fit into my life, especially as they effect my related choices, assumptions and related fears.

These situations where I have been told "no" or showed up and was asked to leave—or even been snubbed along the way—have shaped and enhanced my ability to stand back up and try again. Sure, these situations are humbling and often embarrassing, like the time I stood up to a boss who had promised me many times to move me to a new part of the business with no indicators of doing anything of the sort. Months later, I called him out in front of the team with his boss in the meeting. This is not a suggested or preferred approach. I eventually left his team and decided not to work with him again. I'm sure the feeling was mutual. Even if I was fired, which could have easily happened, it would have been a good lesson and opportunity to grow in new ways because I was beyond my learning curve in that role.

As I look at all my career potholes, detours and promotions, many are great indicators of what I have learned, my blind spots at the time and what was ahead. I have definitely curved my edges along the way and have even grown to recognize that most people are doing the best they can each day, which gives me more empathy and patience with myself. Sure, I still go through times of "poor me" or "there is no way I can do that," but these are much shorter and come with more laughter and insight. When I am feeling like I cannot conquer the task at hand, I visit some of my favorite emails, which I save in a special folder labeled "+" for making me feel good. I also revisit articles such as "10 Famous Failures That Will Inspire You To Be A Success" posted on ASKTEN, International Leadership Consultancy.

I realize now, fear is there all the time. I can choose to feed it or starve it. The more I give myself permission to stretch into unchartered areas, the less likely I am to feed fear as the basis of my decisions. I have a track record of overcoming the unknown, which is often never as bad as I imagined and often fosters new levels of confidence, self-efficacy and opportunities.

With each experience, I have learned to depend on my ability, past experiences and tenacity. I know, despite my nagging fears, if I push forward, I will find a way to deliver results. I'm confident if I cannot do it, it's likely others cannot either, which is echoed in *The Atlantic*'s May 2014 article by Katty Kay and Claire Shipman:

> *Success, it turns out, correlates just as closely with confidence as it does with competence...The good news is that with work, confidence can be acquired.*

In most situations, the positive has almost always outweighed the negative experiences and through these "yeses" I have met fantastic people and surprised myself on what is possible. Through these calculated risks where I have challenged my fears, I have identified new opportunities, been summoned to new networks and been invited to join a few boards as a director.

As we round out this chapter consider your answers to these questions:
- Where do I desire to have more influence and impact in the next 12 months?
- How is fear holding me back?
- What am I afraid of as it relates to my desired next steps?
- Who can I safely share my fears with to help gain perspective and support?
- What small steps can I make in the next eight weeks to increase my confidence?
- Can I arrange a timeline with passable milestones to help gain momentum to push through my fears toward my goals?

- Do I need outside reassurance such as a coach or mentor to help me move toward my goals?
- What will I do differently now that I am aware of these data points and strategies?

EPILOGUE

Reciprocation

With an entire book on strategies for professional women to define, align, position and propel toward a desired goal, I think a good place to end this discussion is with helping others along the way.

As you have witnessed firsthand in many of these chapters, we all need help at one point or another. In fact, many of the strategies and lessons included in this book have been shared with me in person, online or through discussions that have come together in these pages to help professionals accelerate their desired path at work and in life.

It's been called pay it forward or giving someone a leg up, but one thing is for sure, this is not a new concept. As you progress in your career, there will be many people you can help along the way. Just as there have likely been a number of people (perhaps all the way back to your elementary school years) who have given you advice and maybe even helped you with something as simple as making a phone call, writing a reference letter or establishing a connection.

A 2011 *Good Housekeeping* article by Rachel Bowie titled "Indra Nooyi on How to Find Your Voice," states: "The times I feel the greatest are when I'm coaching, developing talent, mentoring people to do what they never thought they could. When you see your team blossoming and growing, you say, 'Man, I'm doing good for the next generation."

If you have a willingness to help, you are already on your way to being a wonderful mentor and maybe even a sponsor for others.

The official Mentor Organization states: "At the most basic level, mentoring helps because it guarantees a person that there is someone who cares about them." That simple feeling of acceptance is so powerful when you're going after a challenge or opportunity that you have confidence you can achieve, but also a little bit of doubt.

Think back to your first few jobs. Did you know how to prepare an important presentation, write your performance review, prepare for a business trip or participate in an executive discussion? Things that we have done often or even seem straightforward may appear to be a hurdle for others.

Mentoring can happen anywhere and sometimes the most rewarding conversations are not even at work. This thought reminds me of a woman I met years ago. She shared a conversation that she had with her exterminator that she now viewed as the catalyst for starting a nonprofit program in her hometown. I share this because not all impactful discussions happen inside your work walls. This woman found guidance and validation from her exterminator. It could have been the right time, right place or it could be numerous other factors that drove her to say "yes" to herself and her idea to move forward. Regardless of this reason, mental stimulation and action-oriented results can manifest from many forms of interactions.

In fact, I have found myself spending time discussing goals and paths forward with my cleaning lady, Chris, as she was looking to expand her business. A neighbor approached me at the mailbox to discuss her plan to prepare for a campaign for a city council seat and even my daughter's friend's mother approached me at Girl Scouts' drop-off as she prepared to re-enter the workforce.

It does not always have to be in a formal setting. These brief meetings could be a phone call or email exchange, and they could be as simple as sharing a reference, website or connection.

Your support and endorsement can act as a multiplier and align to areas you desire to impact too. For example, if you are inspired to advance others in your community, connect with a local college and offer to meet with soon-to-graduate seniors in your area of expertise. Even if you travel for work, you could be available via phone or email to answer their questions, make introductions, offer advice or simply share your experience without even leaving your desk.

Like many of you, I am often crunched for time. I organize some of my events via SKYPE, which has been a fun and effective way to connect with people while I am traveling or locked down in my office meeting deadlines. When I do have the bandwidth to get out, I offer to speak to students at a local college or university in my area of professional expertise. I have also participated in some formal mentorship programs online such as Million Women Mentors.

Million Women Mentors is an organization that supports the engagement of 1 million STEM mentors—male and female—to increase the interest and confidence of girls and women to persist and succeed in STEM programs and careers.

If you are not sure how to initiate a mentoring or sponsor-based relationship, ask around. Many women already mentor the people on their team, which is wonderful, as long as you are not considered the "mother hen" of the group or office. This type of labeling could impact how people view you in the office, which could positively and sometimes negatively impact your brand. Be selective and genuine. Do not feel that you need to take on a whole group or department.

If you are thinking where can I jump in, it might be best to start with your company's HR team. Most companies have a program to connect their employees to a mentee. If your organization or group is looking to organize a formal mentoring initiative consider reading the 2016 Huffington Post article titled "11 Steps to Launching Your Corporate Mentoring Initiative" by Julie Kantor.

Kantor includes great ideas to get employees engaged and excited about connecting and building meaningful professional relationships that can have employee and business benefits. Being a mentor or sponsor can be rewarding. As I look back at the feedback I have received over the years, the general themes have circled around these benefits, which have helped me better understand my brand and my impact:

- Knowledgeable about a particular industry.
- Genuine advice with no hidden agenda.
- Confidential conversations.
- Willingness to listen, guide and share.

What I have learned is that most of us can bring some level of value to almost anyone in our lives. Taking the time to engage people in productive professional discussions is a great way to start.

EXPAND YOUR IMPACT, BE A SPONSOR

Most of us can benefit from others that are willing to spend the time to guide us on our career path. Let's take a minute to talk about how you can nurture your network to be a sponsor for others inside and outside the business world. Matt Cotner wrote an article called "Using Your Centers of Influence" in 2010 suggesting: "Never forget that you, too, can be a center of influence." You are likely involved in groups of people inside or outside of work. Consider how you might leverage these people and opportunities to create momentum for others. You never know what conversation will lead you to an action that connects, sponsors or supports someone within his or her journey.

When I was writing my first book, *The Working Woman's GPS*, I was hosting a daylong conference for women in tech. I received a call from Jill, a woman planning to attend the conference asking me to meet with another woman, Sara, who could benefit from the conference. During this initial call with Jill, I asked about the specific needs of Sara, and she mentioned that she needed some advice on how to get an online business started and how to find trusted development resources.

Jill called me because she knew I had these types of resources in my network. Although I was already overcommitted within an intense tech job while organizing and leading this conference off the side of my desk, I happily found time to give Sara a call.

We had a great conversation. I was surprised to learn of her disability, which prompted her to create her online startup for others that experienced similar challenges online. She was so inspiring, and I was so energized by her tenacity and grit that I gave her a free ticket to the tech conference. I also offered to give her the platform for 15 minutes, unscheduled, where she could share her story and business. Before she walked on stage, I encouraged her to ask for the technical resources she needed to get her online business off the ground.

She wowed the audience with her attitude and the goals for her business. A few attendees connected with her that day to inquire and connect her to some experienced developers. She believed these new connections would likely help her meet her business goals and launch date.

As she was leaving the event, she asked: "How can I help you?" I was not looking for anything in return, but as I was approaching a writing deadline for my first book, I mentioned with no expectations "I may need a book editor." She said, "I cannot think of anyone now, but I will inquire in my network." We exchanged smiles and happily parted ways.

A few weeks later, I received a call from her. Much to my surprise, she was thrilled to share a book editor with me—Deborah Burke. Now most people interview three to five editors before finding the right person. After one call, I knew her recommendation was a good fit. I felt so blessed because it was a good match for me, my voice and my genre. I worked with Deb until my book was published. To this day, I see her as a gift from the universe. She helped me organize my first book, mentored me to stay on track and encouraged me when I second-guessed myself. She was more than an editor—she was a sponsor that lifted me up when I encountered fear, uncertainty and obstacles. I am so grateful for Sara, Jill and Deb. They all were instrumental in my professional journey, which was not initially obvious but looking back on this chain of connection, started based on a request for my time.

Being open to sharing your gifts, connections and network as a mentor or sponsor might bring surprising results. Spend a minute to think about your investment in other people:

• Who am I mentoring or sponsoring now?
• What type of results have I generated during these exchanges?
• Who would I like to mentor in the next six to 12 months? Why?

You know I could not end without sharing another chart to help observe your mentoring and sponsoring activities with areas to capture the related impact.

Person	Their Goals	Meeting Date (in person or virtual)	Your Action Items	Their Next Steps or Results	Level of Impact

If inclined, you can even add an impact scale (1-5) at the end of the chart to determine your level of impact, with 1 indicating a need to invest more in the outcome and 5 indicating gratitude for the exchange/relationship.

Many organizations have used some format of this simple chart to help ensure effective and engaging mentoring sessions. I have shared it with my teams over the years especially as we are working on new initiatives or forming new teams. It has created conversations outside of the project goals that have allowed us to learn about each other first. I believe it has been the catalyst for some of my more successful projects where we have achieved great results with an effective culture of teamwork fostered by empathy and consciousness.

The fun has not stopped there. My kids seem to love the chart and related conversations too—especially as they start project-based activities. They are often involved in community and school-based initiatives where they are working with a variety of other kids. This chart has encouraged my kids to ask other kids about their goals and interests. It seems to stimulate conversation, especially at the start of a new program or initiative, and gets them thinking about how they can help others achieve their goals. They have also found that many kids quickly respond with reciprocal questions inquiring about my kids' goals and how they can help them. As a gushing mom, it is very cute.

From my viewpoint, conversations based on the desire to help others with their goals have generated some great ideas, creative activities, fantastic partnerships and notable outcomes. There are no limits when people are working to genuinely collaborate, which often starts with a simple exchange.

There are numerous quotes to pick from online, but these seemed appropriate:

"Helping others is the secret sauce to a happy life."
Todd Stocker, *Refined: Turning Pain Into Purpose*

"It is literally true that you can succeed best and quickest by helping others to succeed."
Napoleon Hill

It has become clear to me that there is rarely one event, one person or one action that catapults you in the direction of your life purpose. It is more often a series of decisions, actions and connections that accelerate you each day to create the momentum to leap toward your specific areas of influence and impact. I encourage you to seize the path you know is possible.

A Playbook for Professional Women

Expanding Your Sphere of Influence and Impact

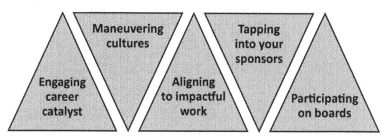

ACCOMPLISHMENTS + CURRENT IMPACT + FUTURE ASPIRATIONS

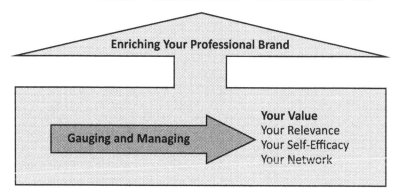

APPENDIX A

PROLOGUE: MAKING YOUR DESIRES KNOWN
Candace Benson. Camp Tech. www.camptechonline.com

Dr. Travis Bradberry. "9 Habits of Profoundly Influential People." LinkedIn: July 19, 2015. www.linkedin.com/pulse/critical-habits-profoundly-influential-people-dr-travis-bradberry

Wikipedia. "Self-efficacy." https://en.wikipedia.org/wiki/Self-efficacy

Wikipedia. "Goal." https://en.wikipedia.org/wiki/Goal

Tara Sophia Mohr. "Why Women Don't Apply for Jobs Unless They're 100% Qualified." Harvard Business Review: Aug 25, 2014. https://hbr.org/2014/08/why-women-dont-apply-for-jobs-unless-theyre-100-qualified

John Bates. "Women Say No." WITI. http://www.witi.com/articles/358/Women-Say-NO

Sylvia Ann Hewlett and Melinda Marshall. "Women Want Five Things." The Center for Talent and Innovation: Dec. 9, 2014. www.talentinnovation.org/_private/assets/WomenWant%20FiveThings_ExecSumm-CTI.pdf

Nina Polien Light. Cleveland Business Connect (CBC): September 2011. www.purposefulwoman.com/wp-content/uploads/2011/09/Cleveland-Business-Connect-September-2011.pdf

CHAPTER 1: PEOPLE, NETWORKS, AND OPPORTUNITIES + HOW READY IS YOUR NETWORK
Monica Biernat, M.J. Tocci, and Joan Williams. "Women in the Workplace: A Research Roundup." Harvard Business Review: September 2013 Issue. https://hbr.org/2013/09/women-in-the-workplace-a-research-roundup

Charles Araujo. "Great IT Leaders Must Be Great Connectors." CIOInsight.com: Aug. 06, 2014. www.cioinsight.com/it-management/expert-voices/great-it-leaders-must-be-great-connectors.html

Anthony Balderrama. "Is getting a job really about who you know?" CareerBuilder.com: September 16, 2010. www.cnn.com/2010/LIVING/09/16/cb.who.you.know/index.html

CHAPTER 2: GAUGING YOUR RELEVANCE
Caroline Dowd-Higgins. "When You Don't Get The Job: 4 Tips To Help You Bounce Back." Caroline blog: April 26, 2015. http://carolinedowdhiggins.com/when-you-dont-get-the-job-4-tips-to-help-you-bounce-back

Pegine Echevarria. "Mentally Tough Woman: An Ongoing Story." LinkedIn: Dec 29, 2014. www.linkedin.com/pulse/mentally-tough-woman-ongoing-story-pegine-echevarria-msw-csp

Dr. Rosenberg's Self-Esteem [Test] highlighted by Debra Stangl, Sedona Soul Adventures blog: April 12, 2015. http://sedonasouladventures.com/2015/04/12/self-esteem-test

Katty Kay and Claire Shipman. The Confidence Code. 2014. http://theconfidencecode.com/books

CHAPTER 3: BUNDLING YOUR VALUE
Glenn Llopis. "5 Common Career Regrets To Avoid." Forbes: Dec 4, 2014. http://www.forbes.com/sites/glennllopis/2014/12/04/5-common-career-regrets-to-avoid/#2df7096826da

Vivian Giang. "The Surprising Ways That Networking Fails Women." Fast Company: March 11, 2015. www.fastcompany.com/3043418/strong-female-lead/the-surprising-ways-that-networking-fails-women

Minda Zetlin. "12 ways women unknowingly sabotage their success." Business Insider: Feb 11, 2015. www.businessinsider.com/ways-women-sabotage-their-success-2015-2

Wendy Capland. *Your Next Bold Move for Women: 9 Proven Steps to Everything You Ever Wanted.* 2013. www.amazon.com/Your-Next-Bold-Move-Women/dp/0985976217

Kieran Snyder. "The resume gap: Are different gender styles contributing to tech's dismal diversity?" Fortune: March 26, 2015. http://fortune.com/2015/03/26/the-resume-gap-women-tell-stories-men-stick-to-facts-and-get-the-advantage

Jody Greene "How to Create an Elevator Pitch." Forbes: Feb. 5, 2015. www.forbes.com/sites/chicceo/2013/02/05/how-to-create-an-elevator-pitch

Nancy Collamer. "The Perfect Elevator Pitch To Land A Job." Forbes: Feb 4, 2013. www.forbes.com/sites/nextavenue/2013/02/04/the-perfect-elevator-pitch-to-land-a-job

Deborah Grayson Riegel. "The Problem With Your Elevator Pitch— And How To Fix It." Fast Company: Jan. 7, 2013. www.fastcompany.com/3004484/problem-your-elevator-pitch-and-how-fix-it

Vanessa Hernandez. "Crafting Your Elevator Speech" Vanessa Renee Hernandez Tumblr: Sept. 3, 2015. http://vanessareneehernandez.tumblr.com/post/125624419540/ramblingscraft-your-elevator-speech

Pamela Wilson. "The Transformative Effect of a Well-Built Brand Statement." CopyBlogger: Sept. 2, 2015. www.copyblogger.com/define-brand-grow-business

CHAPTER 4: BOOSTING YOUR SELF-EFFICACY
Bernard Marr. "The 7 Biggest Excuses That Stop You Succeeding." LinkedIn: March 24, 2015. www.linkedin.com/pulse/7-biggest-excuses-stop-you-succeeding-bernard-marr

Wikipedia. "Self-efficacy." https://en.wikipedia.org/wiki/Self-efficacy

Marissa Levin. "The Three Pillars of Leadership Confidence & How to Build Them." LinkedIn: April 5, 2015. www.linkedin.com/pulse/three-pillars-leadership-confidence-how-build-them-ma-hrd-and-od

Jenna Goudreau. "When Women Feel Like Frauds They Fuel Their Own Failures." Forbes: Oct. 19, 2011. www.forbes.com/sites/jennagoudreau/2011/10/19/women-feel-like-frauds-failures-tina-fey-sheryl-sandberg

Pauline Clance and Suzanne Imes. "Impostor Syndrome." PaulineRoseClance.com: PDF 1978. www.paulineroseclance.com/pdf/ip_high_achieving_women.pdf

Dr. Valerie Young. The Secret Thoughts of Successful Women. 2011. http://impostorsyndrome.com

Mike San Román. "8 Practical Steps to Getting Over Your Impostor Syndrome." Fast Company: Sept. 23, 2014. www.fastcompany.com/3036006/hit-the-ground-running/8-practical-steps-to-getting-over-your-impostor-syndrome

CHAPTER 5: COMPILING YOUR CONNECTIONS AND ACCOMPLISHMENTS

Cathie Ericson. "Voice of Experience: Alaina Percival, CEO, Women Who Code." The Glasshammer: Nov. 2, 2015. http://theglasshammer. com/2015/11/02/voice-of-experience-alaina-percival-ceo-women-who-code

Paul Bray. "Women needed in STEM jobs for the sake of innovation." Telegraph.co.uk: January 5, 2015. www.telegraph.co.uk/sponsored/ education/stem-awards/energy/11325471/women-needed-stem-jobs.html

Business Volunteer Unlimited. www.BVUvolunteers.org

TechSavvyWomen.TV. www.TechSavvyWomen.TV

CHAPTER 6: ENHANCING YOUR PROFESSIONAL BRAND

Wikipedia. "360 reviews." https://en.wikipedia.org/wiki/360-degree_ feedback

Lois P. Frankel, Ph.D. *Nice Girls Don't Get the Corner Office*. 2004. www.amazon.com/Nice-Girls-Dont-Corner-Office/dp/B004PFU7BS

Tory Johnson "Lois Frankel, Nice Girls Don't Get the Corner Office." Women for Hire Website. http://womenforhire.com/advice/lois-frankel-nice-girls-dont-get-the-corner-office

Kevin Gibbons. "SEO Tips For Building Your Personal Brand." Search Engine Optimization (SEO): June 22, 2009. http://searchengineland.com/ seo-tips-for-building-your-personal-brand-21380

Personal Branding Blog. "5 Steps to More Professional Personal Branding." Small Business Trends: May 25, 2015. http://smallbiztrends. com/2015/05/5-tips-professional-personal-branding.html

Joanna Bloor. "Brand and online social networking strategies: which one comes first?" Leading Women in Technology. www.leadingwomenintechnology.org/events/brand

Molly Brown. "How developing a personal brand can help women boost their career potential." Geekwire: Feb.11, 2015. www.geekwire.com/2015/fuel-talent-presents-events-focused-helping-women-boost-career-potential

JJ DiGeronimo "How to make a name for yourself on LinkedIn." JJDiGeronimo.com: August 20, 2015. www.JJDiGeronimo.com/making-a-name-for-yourself-on-linkedin

Mabel Valdiviezo. "How to Reignite Your Personal Power and Branding." Huffington Post Women: Sept. 04, 2015. www.huffingtonpost.com/ellevate/how-to-reignite-your-pers_b_8089958.html

Joanna Bloor. "Wilpower 2015 - Session 4: Developing Your Brand in the Social Media Age." Leading Women in Technology. www.leadingwomenintechnology.org/programs/wilpower/wilpower-2015/networking

CHAPTER 7: TARGETING YOUR RELEVANCE TO ENRICH YOUR BRAND

Susan A. Friedmann, CSP. *Riches in Niches: How to Make It Big in a Small Market*. 2007. www.amazon.com/Riches-Niches-Make-Small-Market/dp/1564149307

Tracy E. Houston. BOARD GURU™. *Final in Trilogy: Becoming a Public Company Director*. (e-book) eBoardmember: June 11, 2015. www.eboardmember.com/1/post/2015/06/board-guru-announces-new-ebook-final-in-trilogy-becoming-a-public-company-director-interview-strategies.html

JJ DiGeronimo. "Power of No." www.JJDiGeronimo.com/no

Brennan Dunn. "Overcoming The Fear Of "Choosing A Niche." Doubling Your Freelancing: April 3, 2015. http://doubleyourfreelancing.com/the-fear-of-niching/

Google Alerts. www.google.com/alerts

Backstitch. http://backstit.ch

Upwork. www.upwork.com

Fiverr. www.fiverr.com

JJ DiGeronimo. *The Working Woman's GPS: When the Plan to Have It All Leads You Astray*. 2011. www.amazon.com/Working-Womans-GPS-Leads-Astray/dp/1935268996

Donné Torr. "The Benefits of LinkedIn Groups and LinkedIn Company Pages (Yes, You Need Both)." HootSuite Blog: Feb. 6, 2015. http://blog.hootsuite.com/linked-groups-vs-linkedin-company-page

Stephanie Sammons. "Why Starting a LinkedIn© Group." Social Media Examiner: Nov. 27, 2012. www.socialmediaexaminer.com/managing-linkedin-groups

CHAPTER 8: FINDING NETWORKING GROUPS THAT WORK FOR YOU
Herminia Ibarra, Robin J. Ely and Deborah M. Kolb. "Women Rising: The Unseen Barriers." Harvard Business Review: September 2013. https://hbr.org/2013/09/women-rising-the-unseen-barriers

Catherine Ashcraft, Ph.D. and Sarah Blithe. "Women in IT: The Facts." The National Center for Women & Information Technology (NCWIT): 2009; updated in April 2010. www.ncwit.org/sites/default/files/legacy/pdf/NCWIT_TheFacts_rev2010.pdf

Sylvia Ann Hewlett, Carolyn Buck Luce, Lisa J. Servon, Laura Sherbin, Peggy Shiller, Eytan Sosnovich, and Karen Sumberg. "The Athena Factor: Reversing the Brain Drain in Science, Engineering, and Technology." New York: Center for Work-Life Policy: June 2008. http://documents.library.nsf.gov/edocs/HD6060-.A84-2008-PDF-Athena-factor-Reversing-the-brain-drain-in-science,-engineering,-and-technology.pdf

Sylvia Ann Hewlett and Laura Sherbin with Fabiola Dieudonne, Christina Fargnoli, and Catherine Fredman. Athena Factor 2.0: Accelerating Female Talent in Science, Engineering & Technology. 2014. www.talentinnovation.org/assets/Athena-2-ExecSummFINAL-CTI.pdf

JJ DiGeronimo. *The Working Woman's GPS: When the Plan to Have It All Leads You Astray.* 2011. www.amazon.com/Working-Womans-GPS-Leads-Astray/dp/1935268996

CHAPTER 9: INVESTING IN YOUR NETWORK
Charles Araujo. "Great IT Leaders Must Be Great Connectors." CIO Insight: Aug. 06, 2014. www.cioinsight.com/it-management/expert-voices/great-it-leaders-must-be-great-connectors.html

Christy Matta. "6 Strategies to Make Valuable Work Connections." Psych Central: Feb. 18, 2013. http://psychcentral.com/blog/archives/2013/02/18/6-strategies-to-make-valuable-work-connections

Kieran Snyder. "The resume gap: Are different gender styles contributing to tech's dismal diversity?" Fortune: March 26, 2015. http://fortune.com/2015/03/26/the-resume-gap-women-tell-stories-men-stick-to-facts-and-get-the-advantage

CHAPTER 10: GETTING THE MOST FROM ORGANIZED EVENTS
Carol Bartz. "Why women should do less and network more." Fortune: Nov. 12, 2014. http://fortune.com/2014/11/12/why-women-should-do-less-and-network-more

Judy Robinett. *How To Be A Power Connector: The 5 + 50 + 150 Rule for Turning Your Business Network into Profits*. 2014. www.judyrobinett.com/book

Madeleine Albright. (n.d.). "I think women are really good at making friends and not good at networking. Men are good at networking and not necessarily making friends. That's a gross generalization, but I think it holds in many ways." BrainyQuote.com. www.brainyquote.com/quotes/quotes/m/madeleinea432620

Stephen Covey. *The 7 Habits of Highly Effective People*. 1990. www.amazon.com/Seven-Habits-Highly-Effective-People/dp/406204983X

Michael Chui, James Manyika, Jacques Bughin, Richard Dobbs, Charles Roxburgh, Hugo Sarrazin, Geoffrey Sands and Magdalena Westergren. "The social economy: Unlocking value and productivity through social technologies." Data by International Data Corporation and the McKinsey Global Institute: July 2012. www.mckinsey.com/industries/high-tech/our-insights/the-social-economy

CHAPTER 11: ENGAGING CATALYSTS: MENTORS, SPONSORS AND ADVISORY BOARDS

Wikipedia. "Social Capital." https://en.wikipedia.org/wiki/Social_capital

Gwen Moran. "Should Women Seek Male Mentors?" Fast Company: Dec. 15, 2014. www.fastcompany.com/3039810/strong-female-lead/should-women-should-seek-male-mentors

CHAPTER 12: IDENTIFYING YOUR SPONSORS

Melissa J. Anderson, Nicki Gilmour, Mekayla Castro. "Women in Technology: Leaders for Tomorrow." Accenture and The Glasshammer published by © Evolved People Media, LLC: 2013. https://acnprod.accenture.com/_acnmedia/Accenture/Conversion-Assets/DotCom/Documents/About-Accenture/PDF/1/Accenture-The-Glass-Hammer-Women-In-Technology-FINAL.pdf

Tech Savvy Women TV "Career Advancement: Networking Advice for Women in Tech." YouTube:March, 10, 2015. www.youtube.com/watch?v=s3UE6-PHc2U

Wikipedia. "Social Capital." https://en.wikipedia.org/wiki/Social_capital

CHAPTER 15: MANEUVERING CULTURES

"5 Things Possessed By Successful Women In IT." CAREEREALISM. www.careerealism.com/successful-women-it

Sylvia Ann Hewlett and Melinda Marshall. "Women Want Five Things." The Center for Talent and Innovation: Dec 9, 2014. www.talentinnovation. org/_private/assets/WomenWant%20FiveThings_ExecSumm-CTI.pdf

Jasmine Tsai. "Stopping Toxicity in Your Engineering Culture." Medium. com: Dec. 29, 2014. https://medium.com/@jasmineyctsai/stopping-toxicity-in-your-engineering-culture-f275753029da#.qn39sci7q

Sylvia Ann Hewlett. "What's Holding Women Back in Science and Technology Industries." Harvard Business Review: March 13, 2014. https://hbr.org/2014/03/whats-holding-women-back-in-science-and-technology-industries

Robin Madell "Should I Stay or Should I Go?" The Glasshammer: Oct. 14, 2014. http://theglasshammer.com/2014/10/14/should-i-stay-or-should-i-go

Bill Murphy Jr. "10 Bad Habits That Make You Look Really Unprofessional." INC: July 8, 2015. http://www.inc.com/bill-murphy-jr/10-bad-habits-that-make-you-look-really-unprofessional.html

CHAPTER 16: ALIGNING TO IMPACTFUL WORK
Rebecca Greenfield. "One Reason Women Aren't Getting the Promotion: They Don't Want It." Bloomberg: Sept. 25, 2015. www.bloomberg.com/news/articles/2015-09-25/women-don-t-want-promotions-as-much-as-men-do

Lois P. Frankel. *Nice Girls Don't Get the Corner Office: 101 Unconscious Mistakes Women Make That Sabotage Their Careers.* 2014 www.amazon.com/Nice-Girls-Dont-Corner-Office/dp/0446531324

Tory Johnson "Lois Frankel, Nice Girls Don't Get the Corner Office." Women for Hire Website. http://womenforhire.com/advice/lois-frankel-nice-girls-dont-get-the-corner-office

Monica Biernat, M.J. Tocci, and Joan Williams. "Women in the Workplace: A Research Roundup." Harvard Business Review: September 2013 Issue. https://hbr.org/2013/09/women-in-the-workplace-a-research-roundup

JJ DiGeronimo. *Before You Say Yes.* (e-book) 2012. www.JJDiGeronimo.com/before-you-say-yes-2

CHAPTER 17: EXPLORING LATERAL MOVES
Kerry Hannon. "Sheryl Sandberg's 5 'Best 'Lean In' Tips For Women." Forbes: March 13, 2013. www.forbes.com/sites/nextavenue/2013/03/13/sheryl-sandbergs-5-best-lean-in-tips-for-women

"Most Powerful Women." Fortune. www.fortune.com/mpw

Joanne Cleaver. "Your Next Job Could Be a Lateral Move – on Your Way to the Top" Next Avenue: August 20, 2012. www.nextavenue.org/your-next-job-could-be-lateral-move--your-way-top

Dawn Dugan. "14 Reasons to Make a Sideways Career Move." Salary.com. www.salary.com/14-reasons-to-make-a-sideways-career-move

Caroline Dowd-Higgins. "How To Recharge, Reignite or Reinvent Your Career" HuffPost Business: Jan. 6, 2015. http://www.huffingtonpost.com/caroline-dowdhiggins/how-to-recharge-reignite-_b_6413458.html

Liz Ryan. "Five Signs Your Job Is Holding You Back." Forbes: Dec. 5, 2015. www.forbes.com/sites/lizryan/2015/12/05/five-signs-your-job-is-holding-you-back

Liz Wiseman. "How to stay excited about your career?" Fortune: Nov. 11, 2014. http://fortune.com/2014/11/11/how-to-stay-excited-about-your-career-never-take-a-job-youre-qualified-for

CHAPTER 18: MAXIMIZING RISK AND MINIMIZING FEARS

Katty Kay and Claire Shipman. The Confidence Gap The Atlantic: May 2014 Issue. www.theatlantic.com/features/archive/2014/04/the-confidence-gap/359815/

Meg Duffy. "3 Steps For Bridging "The Confidence Gap." 99U. http://99u.com/articles/40205/3-steps-for-bridging-the-confidence-gap

Carol Sankar. "Shattering the "Glass Ceiling" Mindset." LinkedIn: Jan 5, 2015. www.linkedin.com/pulse/shattering-glass-ceiling-mindset-carol-sankar

Robin Madell. "Overcome Fears to Do Better at Work." U.S. News & World Report: March 23, 2015. http://money.usnews.com/money/blogs/outside-voices-careers/2015/03/23/overcome-fears-to-do-better-at-work

Gail Sheehy. Passages: Predictable Crises of Adult Life. 1976. www.amazon.com/Passages-Predictable-Crises-Adult-Life/dp/034547922X

Gail Sheehy. Daring: My Passages. 2014. www.amazon.com/Daring-Passages-Memoir-Gail-Sheehy/dp/0062291696

"10 Famous Failures That Will Inspire You To Be A Success." askten, Leadership development and talent management consultancy: June 28, 2015. http://askten.co.uk/resources/article/643/10-famous-failures-will-inspire-you-be-success

EPILOGUE: RECIPROCATION

Rachel Bowie. "Indra Nooyi on How to Find Your Voice." Good Housekeeping: Aug. 5, 2011. www.goodhousekeeping.com/life/inspirational-stories/a18931/indra-nooyi-blogher

"Most Powerful Woman" Fortune. http://fortune.com/most-powerful-women

Mentor organization. www.mentoring.org/about_mentor/value_of_mentoring

Million Women Mentors. www.millionwomenmentors.org

The Mentoring Women's Network. www.linkedin.com/company/mentoring-women%27s-network

Julie Kantor. "11 Steps to Launching Your Corporate Mentoring Initiative." Huffington Post: Jan. 5, 2016. www.huffingtonpost.com/julie-kantor/11-steps-to-launching-you_b_8911418.html

Matt Cotner. "Using Your Centers of Influence Following Three Simple Steps." EzineArticles.com: April 14, 2010. http://ezinearticles.com/?Using-Your-Centers-of-Influence-Following-Three-Simple-Steps&id=4113449

Todd Stocker. *Refined: Turning Pain Into Purpose*. GoodReads.com. www.goodreads.com/work/quotes/21625513

Napoleon Hill. GoodReads.com. www.goodreads.com/quotes/3206100-it-is-literally-true-that-you-can-succeed-best-and

APPENDIX B

Abbreviated List of Organizations, From Chapter 8

WOMEN'S ORGANIZATIONS (NATIONAL)

American Business Women's Association, www.abwa.org
Athena International, www.athenainternational.org
Working Women Connection,
www. workingwomenconnection.com
National Association of Women Business Owners,
www.nawbo.org
National Association of Female Executives, www.nafe.com
American Business Women's Association, www.abwa.org
National Association of Professional Women, www.napw.org
The Glasshammer, http://theglasshammer.com
YWCA, www.ywca.org
WirL, www.wirlsummit.com

WOMEN IN TECHNOLOGY

Anita Borg Institute, www.anitaborg.org
CodeChix, www.codechix.org
Global Tech Women, www.globaltechwomen.com
Million Women Mentors, www.millionwomenmentors.org
NCWIT, www.ncwit.org
NPower, www.npower.org
Pink Petro, www.pinkpetro.com
STEM Connectors, www.stemconnector.org
Tech Savvy Women LLC, www.TechSavvyWomen.net
WITI, www.witi.com
Women in AV, www.womeninav.com

GIRLS INTERESTED IN TECHNOLOGY, MATH AND SCIENCE

CampTech, www.Camptechonline.com

DigiGirlz (Microsoft), www.microsoft.com/en-us/diversity/programs/digigirlz

Expanding Your Horizon (AT&T), www.eyhn.org

Gems Club: Girls Excelling in Math and Science, www.gemsclub.org

Girl Geeks, www.girlgeeks.org

Girl Scouts, www.girlscouts.org/program/basics/science

Girls Inc., www.girlsinc.org

Girls Who Code, www.girlswhocode.com

Girls-ology, www.girlsology.com

ID Tech, www.idtech.com

National Girls Collaboration, www.ngcproject.org

Project Lead the Way, www.pltw.org

Sally Ride Science, www.sallyridescience.com

STEM.org, www.stem.org

STEMgeo, www.stemgeo.com

Tech Bridge, www.techbridgegirls.org

Tech Girls, www.legacyintl.org

TechPREP, www.techprepnwo.org

We Can Code IT, www.wecancodeit.org

Youth Campaign, http://youthcampaigns.org

APPENDIX C

Condensed List of Tech Savvy Women Videos

"A Diverse Board, Key Influencer: Valerie Jennings Shares her Professional Advice," https://youtu.be/ilXyu5oE5Z8

"A Woman Engineer: Making a Solar Impact on the World, Eden Full (Woman in STEM)," https://youtu.be/krVU6G0aFkI

"Advice for Career Women: Passion Drives Action, This is not a dress-rehearsal!," https://youtu.be/ABVOgcaFGfI

"App Entrepreneur at 15 Yrs. Old: Superstar Megan Holstein is the CEO of Pufferfish Software," https://youtu.be/wv8bUHzwkCc

"Career Advancement: Networking Advice for Women in Tech," https://youtu.be/s3UE6-PHc2U

"Career Advice: 10 Career Potholes to Avoid," https://youtu.be/Qddp-l33ntw

"Career Advice: Before You Quit A Bad Manager," https://youtu.be/8xdoUqIi0pM

"Career Advice: Delegating Your Way to Success with Lisa Crilley Mallis," https://youtu.be/3TS15vZVHfw

"Career Women: Embracing Change," https://youtu.be/MKBPFsAXbfg

"Career Women: Stretching Your Skills," https://youtu.be/rrFW8Qsl0Ew

"Changes at Work: How to handling unwelcome Workplace Transitions," https://youtu.be/YuqEEhk2D3E

"Changing Jobs: Common Resume Questions,"
https://youtu.be/EllYhEnE7us

"Dynamic Career: With a Bachelors in Mathematics, Karen Sands,
Women in STEM," https://youtu.be/hKKN7cxSHdA

"Executive Woman in Tech: Technology Delivery, Thanh Hua,"
https://youtu.be/rAKxb6QlTNs

"Finding a Job: Resume Requirements based on Your Expertise!,"
https://youtu.be/blQLCMyFd_M

"Get Your Business Started: 3 Things to Do Today,"
https://youtu.be/9HXmW1JJazs

"Girl in STEM: Future Engineer, Emily Liptow, STEM College Student,"
https://youtu.be/HDZKES1xn1Y

"Interview Advice: Be the Final Candidate,"
https://youtu.be/Jtyj9QiZCQw

"Leadership for Women: 3 Easy Ways to Stay Relevant in Your Career,"
https://youtu.be/Ss_mKigOKYc

"Leadership for Women: Energy Vampires at Work, Conquer with Grace,
Betsy Muller," https://youtu.be/p4hE7IFFiGk

"Leadership for Women: Exploring New Roles After Making
a Professional Commitment," https://youtu.be/f1_lDiIoTbo

"Leadership for Women: Quick Tips to Define Your Business Value?,"
https://youtu.be/ujVcSoeNFvM

"Leadership for Women: Real Results Matter for Professional Women,"
https://youtu.be/If5GS4l-Kos

"Leadership Strategies: Professional Women looking for More Influence
& Impact?," https://youtu.be/u5r1TeOPoQ8

"New Boss: Create A Positive Impression with Betsy Muller,"
https://youtu.be/z77mOxiWTKA

"Resume Advice: How do I incorporate these my education credentials
into my resume?," https://youtu.be/kfgk-UV3hoc

"Resume Advice: Objective Statement, What should I do with 'this' in my
Resume?," https://youtu.be/wrIwAE5TD4A

"Resume Advice: Headers, Dos and Don'ts of Resume Headers,"
https://youtu.be/rNZaxSlD118

"Resume Advice: How do I incorporate many jobs into my resume?,"
https://youtu.be/ozn0M61SH_0

"Resume Advice: References, Where do they go on my resume?,"
https://youtu.be/JsSn0hT0CMk

"Retaining Women: Don't Quit, Stay Involved, Consider
Entrepreneurship!," https://youtu.be/1-VkCM6nuLA

"Successful Woman: Web Designer & Mom Doing It All! Women
in STEM Series," https://youtu.be/do1iTbYtanA

"Tech Girls: Are SUPERHEROES with Jenine Beekhuyzen,"
https://youtu.be/j6dKXjL8GSc

"Tech Woman: Builds Website to Raising Mindful Kids through
Family Trips—Our Whole Village," https://youtu.be/wpvKrrxTNvs

"Thought Diversity: Jack Welch's Insight to Executive Diversity,"
https://youtu.be/IBpczBuHdhs

"Virtual Incubator for Technology Companies: Founder Sramana Mitra,
Women in STEM Video," https://youtu.be/1rWfWYuIPSc

"Woman Aerospace Engineer: Natalie Panek, Woman in STEM,
joins us from Canada," https://youtu.be/IzqPjohHTJg

"Woman Author: Dreams, Turn Your Dreams into Reality!,"
https://youtu.be/nJJHQXBbc-c

"Woman CIO: Delivering IT Services, Women in STEM—Laura Pettit Rusick,"
https://youtu.be/ZD0rv4BUDk0

"Woman Developer: Women in STEM: Tech Mothers' Podcast,
The Motherboard Podcast," https://youtu.be/z8rFJ-PCmts

"Woman in Aerospace and Defense: Women in STEM, Shirley Troilo,"
https://youtu.be/SOOCPiekXGk

"Woman in Tech: Woman Leader = Leading EDJE LLC, Erica Krumlauf's
Journey in STEM," https://youtu.be/C2ikVPoNedk

"Woman in Tech: Savita Thakur Love, STEM Careers for Women,"
https://youtu.be/yLR9w3OfaWg

"Women in Tech: IP & Technology Transfer Firm Expert, Laura Schoppe President at Fuentek LLC," **https://youtu.be/Fg8rTUnzVqk**

"Women in Tech: Global Business Woman Living in Dubai, after working with Clinton's Foundation," **https://youtu.be/_OhQGMJLrEU**

"Working Women: Strategies to be Happier at Work," **https://youtu.be/eMsvbag8EQs**

ABOUT THE AUTHOR

JJ DIGERONIMO, president of Tech Savvy Women, is one of the most highly regarded speakers, authors and executive strategists to attract, retain and advance professional women in technology and related fields. Through her keynotes and executive sessions, JJ shares effective leadership and inclusion strategies to retain and develop diverse talent. Her work is featured in *Forbes* and The Wall Street Journal, along with many other publications.

JJ began her career designing computer infrastructures for *Fortune* 500 companies after graduating with a computer information systems degree in 1995. She stays involved with emerging technologies, as she is a strategic adviser to venture capitalists, investment teams and executives as it relates to routes-to-market and repeatable revenue streams.

With 20 years of experience in high tech, JJ advanced from entry-level technology positions into leadership positions within Silicon Valley-based technology companies. Recently, JJ completed eight years at VMware, where she focused on data center technologies: cloud computing, virtualization and SDDC.

JJ is now a featured columnist for *Smart Business*, a regular guest on TV and radio shows and a speaker for many corporate events including Amazon, Ingram Micro, RIT, Cisco, Sears Holding Co., Clemson University, Symantec, VMware, Grace Hopper, KeyBank, EMC and many other organizations.

She includes these experiences along with hours of leadership research in her book, *The Working Woman's GPS*. She also contributed to the book, *The Confident Woman: Tapping Into Your Inner Power* and hosts regular videos on www.TechSavvyWomen.TV.

Throughout her career, JJ has made a positive impact within the technology industry. Her accomplishments and contributions include:

- Top 100 Women Visionary Leaders To Watch In 2016, Innov8tiv, 2016
- JumpStart board member, nonprofit Accelerator for High Growth Companies, 2015
- Strategic adviser for STEMPoweredKids, CoolTechGirls and Her Ideas in Motion, 2014
- Initiated "What DO Women in STEM DO?" video channel, 2013
- Named to Top 25 People in Technology by *Inside Business*, Cleveland
- Next Generation Indie Book Award for *The Working Woman's GPS*, 2011
- Co-creator of Diversity Corporate Initiative Women on Purpose at VMware, to empower and advance women in the technology industry, 2009
- Launched Tech Savvy Women, an experienced network of women in tech and related fields, 2008
- Innovation Award from the *Small Business*, 2005
- *Entrepreneur Magazine* featured her company, TechStudents, the largest database of technology graduates from 300 colleges and universities, 2004

TECH SAVVY WOMEN: EXPERIENCED WOMEN IN TECH, CREATING A COMPETITIVE ADVANTAGE

Tech *Savvy* Women

Tech Savvy Women LLC is a firm that works to attract, retain, celebrate and promote experienced women in technology and related industries. Since its inception, Tech Savvy Women has hosted hundreds of events for professional women in technology.

Additionally, the company facilitates recruiting and retention sessions for executives and organizational leaders looking to interlock their diverse talent with business value.

Tech Savvy Women members share a wealth of knowledge, experience and value with thousands of Women in Tech representing various industries and technical disciplines.

STAY IN TOUCH

What I have learned throughout my career is that people don't fall into great positions, roles or opportunities. These opportunities come after you have stretched yourself to access the next level of your courage, risk-taking, perseverance and willingness to manifest what you desire. Through these decisions, actions and interactions, I hope you have the momentum and acceleration to catapult forward.

I hope this book has inspired you to accelerate what you know is possible.

I would love to read about your experiences and feedback as it relates to this book and even welcome you to continue the journey with us by participate in our online groups, in-person events or offline discussions.

Visit our websites: www.TechSavvyWomen.net and
www.JJDiGeronimo.com
View our video channel: www.TechSavvyWomen.TV
Contact us: contact@techsavvywomen.net
Join our LinkedIn Group: Tech Savvy Women
Like our Facebook Page: www.facebook.com/techsavvywomen